Praise for The Conflict of the Ages Series

" ... Great to teach about creation and that theory ... religious approach more then the scinetific but I want my children to know both and make up their minds."

" ... Exceptionally well researched and superbly informative ... "

" ... Should be required reading for every college bound teenager ... "

"I can't wait to dive into volume two."

The Conflict of the Ages
Part Two, Teacher Edition
The Origin of Evil in the World that Was

by

Michael J. and Mary C. Findley

Findley Family Video Publications

The Conflict of the Ages Part Two, Teacher Edition The Origin of Evil in the World that Was

Any images not sourced in the text are from Public Domain sources or the authors' personal collection.

"Speaking the truth in love."

Table of Contents

End of Main Text

Unclean Spirits: The Oldest Recorded Evil

I. Unclean Spirits: The Oldest Recorded Evil

And God saw everything that he had made, and, behold, it was very good. And the evening and the morning were the sixth day. (Genesis 1:31) *Conflict of the Ages Part One: The Scientific History of Origins* concludes with the creation completed. The original Creation, including spiritual beings, was created "very good."

At some point during this creation, God created the being described below.

Lucifer, The Leader of Unclean Spirits

A. Lucifer, The Leader of Unclean Spirits

" ... *You were the seal of perfection, full of wisdom and perfect in beauty. You were in Eden, the garden of God; every precious stone adorned you: carnelian, chrysolite and emerald, topaz, onyx and jasper, lapis lazuli, turquoise and beryl. Your settings and mountings were made of gold; on the day you were created they were prepared. You were anointed as a guardian cherub, for so I ordained you. You were on the holy mount of God; you walked among the fiery stones. You were blameless in your ways from the day you were created* ... " (Ezekiel 28:11-19, NASB)

1. The Anointed Cherub

Like all the other created things, this being was created "very good." Lucifer, or Satan, was created as a cherub before God created the man, Adam. Lucifer walked in Eden. He walked in stones of fire (probably volcanic activity in or near the garden of Eden), and was adorned in gold and jewels. But Ezekiel continues.

> *"... till wickedness was found in you. Through your widespread trade you were filled with violence, and you sinned. So I drove you in disgrace from the mount of God, and I expelled you, guardian cherub, from among the fiery stones. Your heart became proud on account of your beauty, and you corrupted your wisdom because of your splendor. So I threw you to the earth; I made spectacle of you before kings. By your many sins and dishonest trade you have desecrated your sanctuaries. So I made a fire come out from you, and it consumed you, and I reduced you to ashes on the ground in the sight of all who were watching. All the nations who know you are appalled at you; you have come to a horrible end and will be no more."*

2. Star of the Morning; Son of the Dawn

Isaiah also describes the same being. Because the Hebrew words can be legitimately translated more than one way, compare the KJV and the NASB. Each translation is correct, but each translation brings out another facet of meaning.

> *How art thou fallen from heaven, O Lucifer, son of the morning! how art thou cut down to the ground, which didst weaken the nations! For thou hast said in thine heart, I will ascend into heaven, I will exalt my throne above the stars of God: I will sit also upon the mount of*

> *the congregation, the sides of the north: I will ascend above the clouds; I will be like the most High. Yet thou shalt be brought down to hell, to the sides of the pit.* (Isaiah 14:12-15 KJV)
>
> *"How you have fallen from heaven, O star of the morning son of the dawn: You have been cut down to the earth, You who have weakened the nations! But you said in your heart, 'I will ascend to heaven; I will raise my throne above the stars of God, and I will sit on the mount of assembly in the north. I will ascend above the height of the clouds; I will make myself like the Most High.'*
>
> *"Nevertheless, you will be thrust down to Sheol, to the recesses of the pit. Those who see you will gaze at you, they will ponder over you, saying, 'Is this the man who made the earth tremble, who shook kingdoms, who made the world like a wilderness and overthrew its cities, who did not allow his prisoners to go home?'"* (Isaiah 14:12-17, NASB)

Both translations are valid. The KJV translates *O Lucifer, son of the morning* as a name and a title. The NASB translates the same Hebrew words as *O star of the morning son of the dawn,* and as a title only.

3. His Power and Authority

The phrase *King of Tyre* in Ezekiel 28:12 is the idea of a clan chieftain, a chosen leader over a group of tribes of equal authority, like David was as the king of Israel. The King of Tyre is not an absolute monarch like Pharaoh, the King of Assyria, the King of Babylon, or the Lord God Almighty. So even though the entire realm of rebellious angels, demons, and unclean spirits united in rebellion against God, they are only kept in line by force. They seem to all want to act independently.

B. The Origin of Unclean Spirits

The KJV translates Ezekiel 28:14, *Thou art the anointed cherub that covereth,* as a title, and he is sometimes called “the Covering Cherub”. He walked upon the holy mountains of God and among the fiery stones. So Satan or Lucifer is the first or leader of these evil spirits.

1. Rebellious or Fallen Angels

Though we have no time reference, at some time Satan deceived a third of the angels into joining him in rebelling against God.

a. Scriptural teaching

This rebellion is described in Revelation.

> *And there appeared another wonder in heaven; and behold a great red dragon, having seven heads and ten horns, and seven crowns upon his heads. And his tail drew the third part of the stars of heaven, and did cast them to the earth.* (Revelation 12:3, 4 KJV)

> *Then another sign appeared in heaven: and behold, a great red dragon having seven heads and ten horns, and on his heads were seven diadems. And his tail swept away a third of the stars of heaven and threw them to the earth.* (Revelation 12:3,4a, NASB)

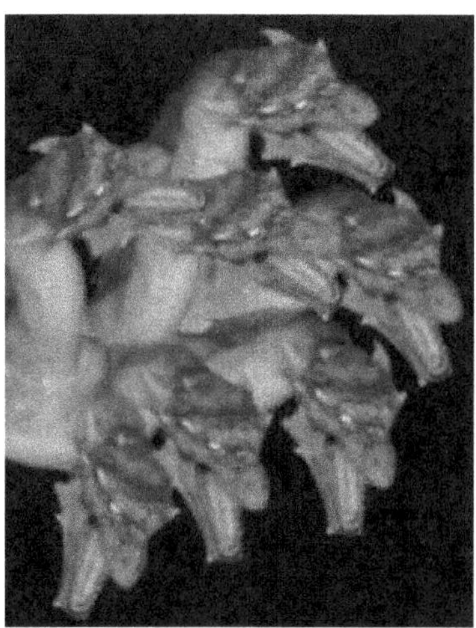

Seven-headed dragon Image made with DAZ 3D program

These Scriptures make the point of Satan's rebellion and sin, as well as his enticing other angels to follow his example. The heavenly beings we call angels come in different varieties. Cherubim, seraphim, angels, archangels are all named in the Scriptures.

Archangel Michael, Kiev, Russia, Public Domain

But it is interesting to compare non-biblical texts that also speak of a proud rebel in ancient times. The cuneiform tablets of the Assyrian people are among the oldest surviving documents in the world.

b. Similarities to the Biblical Record in Other Sources

Translator George Smith, author of *The Chaldean Account of Genesis*,[1] includes in his work a translation from Assyrian cuneiform tablets that he admits are fragmentary and which he does not fully understand. He calls this story "The Sin of Zu." (Question marks in quoted texts refer to words the translator is uncertain about.)

> 9. The desire(?) of majesty he conceived in his heart,
> 14. may my throne be established, may I possess the parzi,
> 15. may I govern the whole of the seed of the angels.
> 16. And he hardened his heart to make war,
> 22. Zu fled away and in his country concealed himself.
> 23. Then spread darkness, and made a commotion ...[1]

Notice the similarities between what the Scriptures teach us about Satan and the Assyrian Zu. Satan rebelled, and led a rebellion of other created beings, because he was proud and wanted to be "like the most high". We are not told if these angels who followed Satan in rebellion are the same as the unclean spirits or demons the New Testament describes, which can inhabit and control men. This is possible.

2. Nephilim

There is a theory concerning the "Sons of God" described in Genesis 6:2, beings who are described as having gone in to the daughters of men before the Flood and produced Nephilim (giants) as offspring. If they were rebellious or fallen angels they may have become demons when their bodies were destroyed in the flood. (Please see a discussion of the alternate theories for the identities of the "sons of god" later in this work.) It is also possible that we know nothing of the origins of demons. Whatever their origins, the Scriptures teach that there are myriads of evil spirits.

C. The Agenda of Unclean Spirits

1. I Will Make Myself Like the Most High

a. Authority of Scripture

Once again, the Scriptures speak for themselves and have authority without any need for "support" from other ancient sources. Still, it is beneficial to examine parallels in other ancient documents, especially those documents claiming to be a record of times before the flood. These documents indicate that all men once knew the truth of God's Word. Without the knowledge of the Word of God, filtering the truth from myths is a hopeless task.

b. Similarities to the Biblical Record in Other Sources

Later in this work (p. 194) we will examine more closely the real origin of legends of gods and demigods. The *Epic of Atrahasis,* an ancient Akkadian account of preflood times, speaks of "lesser gods" attacking and trying to overthrow "greater gods". The lesser gods resented being made to do all the work of digging canals and growing food. (The endnote also sources the text in the graphic below.)[2]

"Let us face up to our foreman the prefect; he must take off our heavy burden upon us! Enlil, counsellor of the gods, the warrior, come, let us remove him from his dwelling."
Background image Public Domain

2. Satan; the Accuser of the Brothers, the Busy One

The account above seems to describe either Satan's original rebellion against God, or perhaps the unrest Satan has to deal with among his rebellious angels. This clearly shows powerful, rebellious spirits that cannot be taken lightly. Not only are they powerful and rebellious, they are in places of authority. Today Satan has access to the very throne of God.

> *Now there was a day when the sons of God came to present themselves before the LORD, and Satan came also among them. And the LORD said unto Satan, Whence comest thou? Then Satan answered the LORD, and said, From going to and fro in the earth, and from walking up and down in it.* (Job 1:6,7 KJV)

Satan's answer, *From going to and fro in the earth, and from walking up and down in it* shows Satan's industry. This is the basis for his name "The busy one." In most non-western cultures he also has a variety of names meaning the industrious, busy one. He is too busy for God. Yet for all his industry, Satan's war on God will not prevail.

II. God's Purpose in Allowing Evil

A God's Plan for Defeating Satan

Satan's Attack: God's Provision

1. The Fall: the Protoevangelium

Satan believed he defeated God by seducing Eve in the Garden. God intervened with the curse, the Fall, expulsion from the garden and the promise of the Messiah.

2. The Flood: the Covenant with Noah

Satan believed he defeated God corrupting the whole earth. God intervened by destroying mankind with a flood while rescuing Noah.

3. The Tower of Babel: the Division of Mankind

Satan then believed that he had united mankind in rebellion against God by building a tower (gate) at Babel. God intervened by dividing mankind though language barriers.

4. National Idolatry: Call of Abraham, Isaac, and Israel

Satan corrupts mankind scattered throughout the earth. God calls Abram. Satan attempts to destroy

Abraham and his children, but fails. Satan believes Joseph dead. God makes Joseph ruler of Egypt.

5. Slavery In Egypt: Moses, the Exodus, and the Law

Satan believes the Children of Israel will be destroyed in Egypt. God sends Moses, destroys Egypt, and gives Canaan to the Israelites.

6. Every man did the Right In His Own Eyes: the Judges

Satan corrupts the Children of Israel repeatedly. God sends Judges, the last being Samuel. Samuel anoints Saul and David, beginning the Kingdom.

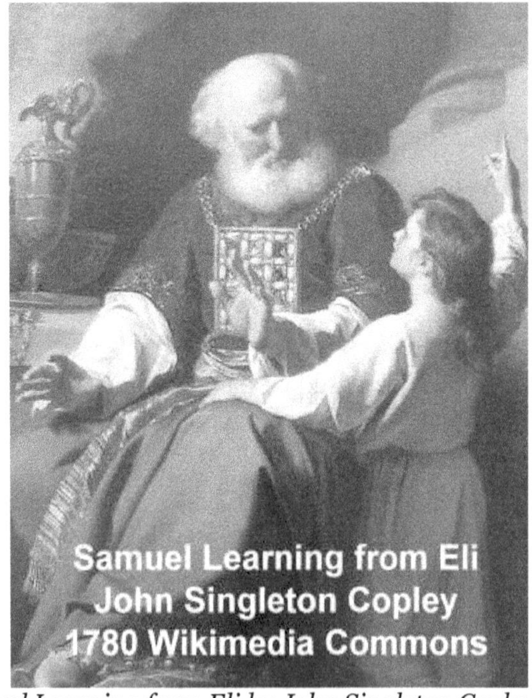

Samuel Learning from Eli by John Singleton Copley 1780 Wikimedia Commons

7. Foreign invaders: God anoints a king

Satan attempts to completely annihilate the Children of Israel using the Philistines, Ammonites, and Amalakites. God sends Saul and David to militarily defeat them.

8. Satan corrupts the kingdom: God sends prophets

Beginning with Solomon's foreign (unbelieving) wives, Satan corrupts the Kings of Israel. God sends his prophets.

9. Israel/Judah reject the prophets: God sends captivity

Satan introduced Baal worship to Israel. God sends Elijah and Elisha. Satan introduces all the gods of the heathens to Judah. God sends Isaiah and Jeremiah.

10. Satan builds World Empires: God sends His Son

Satan builds the Empires of World; Babylon, Persia, Greece and Rome. God sends His Son.

11. The Church corrupted: Rapture and Tribulation

Satan corrupts the Church: God removes His Church and sends Great Tribulation on Earth, temple is rebuilt and sacrifices restarted.

12. Satan attacks Israel: Messiah returns/Satan bound

Satan attacks Israel directly: Jesus returns and set up His Kingdom on Earth. Satan is bound for a thousand years.

13. Satan released: Eternal judgment

Satan is released and deceives the entire world once again into attacking God: God destroys the Universe with judgment and eternity begins.

B. Satan's Future

1. Satan will be thrown out of heaven.

Today Satan is known as the Prince (or ruler) of the Power (or authority or power of choice) of the Air.

a. Satan made accountable for bringing sin into the universe

Satan is responsible for sin. He introduced sin into the material universe by deceiving Eve. These judgments on Satan are the consequences of the decisions Satan made.

There is no way to know if the angels (called "stars" in Revelation 12:3-4, quoted above) were with Satan in Eden. We know that Satan wanted to be like the Most High. After his own fall, it appears that the first step Satan took to again attempt to "be like the Most High" was to corrupt God's crowning achievement, the being created to worship God and to fellowship with Him: man.

Lucifer, the Light-Bearer, Son of the Dawn, became Satan, the Devil, and the great Red Dragon. Sin originated with Satan in his rebellion against God, his pride and his seeking to get followers and worshipers. Through Adam, the first man to sin, sin crossed the boundary from the spiritual world to the material universe. Satan is also known as the accuser, because of his fondness for pointing out man's sin, the sin he led man into.

b. Satan and his angels will live on the material earth

Sometime in the future, Satan and his angels will be thrown out of heaven. Since this is before they are thrown into the Lake of Fire, at that time they will live on the Earth. When Satan and his angels are cast out into the earth, the earth might mean just planet Earth or it might mean the entire material universe. This passage in Revelation describes the banishment from heaven of Satan and his angels.

> *And there was war in heaven: Michael and his angels fought against the dragon; and the dragon fought and his angels, and prevailed not; neither was their place found any more in heaven. And the great dragon was cast out, that old serpent, called the Devil, and Satan, which deceiveth the whole world: he was cast out into the earth, and his angels were cast out with him.* (Revelation 12:7-9)

Public Domain Image Statue of Michael Defeating Satan

2. Satan will be in the Abyss for one thousand years

When Jesus the Messiah returns to earth in power and glory, his feet will touch the Mount of Olives and Satan will be cast into what is called the bottomless pit in the

KJV but is called the abyss in most translations. The bottomless pit or the abyss is not the Lake of Fire. The beast and the false prophet will be thrown immediately into their eternal dwelling the Lake of Fire. Satan will be released from the bottomless pit after one thousand years to travel about on the earth.

Then I saw an angel coming down from heaven, holding the key of the abyss and a great chain in his hand. And he laid hold of the dragon, the serpent of old, who is the devil and Satan, and bound him for a thousand years; and he threw him into the abyss, and shut it and sealed it over him, so that he would not deceive the nations any longer, until the thousand years were completed; after these things he must be released for a short time. (Revelation 20:1-3 NASB)

3. Satan will be in the dark Lake of Fire for eternity

wandering stars, to whom is reserved the blackness of darkness for ever. (Jude 13 KJV)

The term "wandering stars" refers to unclean spirits. Just as there are categories of angels so there are categories of unclean spirits.

When the thousand years are completed, Satan will be released from his prison, and will come out to deceive the nations which are in the four corners of the earth, Gog and Magog, to gather them together for the war; the number of them is like the sand of the seashore. And they came up on the broad plain of the earth and surrounded the camp of the saints and the beloved city, and fire came down from heaven and devoured them. And the devil who deceived them was thrown into the lake of fire and brimstone, where the beast and the false prophet are also; and they will be tormented day and night forever and ever. (Revelation 20:7-10 NASB)

C. The Origin of Evil

To properly understand the origin of evil, we must understand several very difficult facts.

1. God did not create evil.

For the wrath of God is revealed from heaven against all ungodliness and unrighteousness of men who suppress the truth in unrighteousness, because that which is known about God is evident within them; for God made it evident to them. For since the creation of the world His invisible attributes, His eternal power and divine nature, have been clearly seen, being understood through what has been made, so that they are without excuse. For even though they knew God, they did not honor Him as God or give thanks, but they became futile in their speculations, and their foolish heart was darkened. Professing to be wise, they became fools... Romans 1:18-22 NASB

2. God created a being, perfect in beauty. This being chose to rebel.

All things came into being through [Jesus] Him, and apart from Him nothing came into being that has come into being. John 1:3 NASB

3. That being, Satan, created by the Messiah, introduced sin into the universe.

You are of your father the devil, and you want to do the desires of your father. He was a murderer from the beginning, and does not stand in the truth because there is no truth in him. Whenever he speaks a lie, he speaks from his own nature, for he is a liar and the father of lies. (John 8:44 NASB)

"You are of your father the devil, and you want to do the desires of your father. He was a murder from the beginning, and does not stand in the truth because there is no truth in him. Whenever he speaks a lie, he speaks from his own nature, for he is a liar, and the father of lies." (John 8:44 NASB)

This verse is included because it teaches us that Satan is the father of lies. But apart from our adoption into a new family, each of us must realize that these words of Jesus apply to us. Our father is the devil. We lie because our father is *the father of lies*. Our father *was a murder from the beginning and does not stand in the truth*. If we do not choose the adoption into the kingdom of God, we will perish with our father, the devil.

4. We do not know why God created Satan.

Many have asked why God created Satan. God does not choose to reveal to us in the Scriptures why he created Satan. This is a very unsatisfying answer, but it is the real answer. The LORD God is sovereign, holy, just, and righteous. Why a holy and just God would create this being, knowing that Satan would plunge, not just the material world, but also the spiritual realms, into chaos, is beyond our ability to understand.

We must rely on Deuteronomy 29:29. *The secret things belong to the LORD our God, but the things revealed belong to us and to our sons forever, that we may observe all the words of this law.* (NASB) After all that we have written so far in this work, we have to admit that the reason for the creation of an anointed cherub that covered, whom God foreknew would rebel and become the ultimate cause of evil, is not knowable.

"The Sin of the God Zu" (from The Chaldean Account of Genesis) includes statements quoted below that make it clear that Zu's evil desires did not originate with his creator ("his mother had not placed him", "his father had not placed him") His actions were a result of his own choices, and his decision to rebel and to deceive mankind came from his own will and heart. (The endnote also sources the quote in the graphic below.)[3]

Whether the passage fits Satan or some human or "demigod" ruler, it is evidence that evil did not originate with God but was a personal act of rebellion. Note also, here and in other ancient texts, that changing into animal or part-animal forms appear in close association with sin and rebellion. This is important to remember, whether Satan actually assumed the form of the serpent, or even if he only indwelt the serpent or controlled its actions.

These passages relate a common theme, that of a powerful being as the source of pride and rebellion, and the original source of evil. Many religions, such as Zoroastrianism, spend enormous amounts of time and energy attempting to determine the origin of evil. Ancient Sanskrit texts of Hinduism contain billions of words on this subject and span centuries of man's written thoughts. Yet these massive tomes shed no more light on the subject. They prove once again that man's reasoning apart from God's revelation does not provide answers.

3. His mother had not placed him
4. his father had not placed him
and with him did not [go],
5. the strength of his knowledge ...
6. From the will of his heart
a resolution he did ...
7. In his own heart a resolution he made,
8. to the likeness of a bird he changed,
9. to the likeness of the divine
storm bird (or Zu bird) he changed,

"his mother had not placed him ... his father had not placed him ... and with him did not {go}, the strngth of his knowledge ... from the will of his heart a resolution he did ... In his own heart a resolution he made, to the likeness of a bird he changes, to the likeness of the divne storm bird (or Zu bird) he changed ..."

D. Love Conquers Evil and Glorifies God

But God did not intend for us to be obsessed with evil; to exhaustively study it. Instead the Word of God commands us to love and worship Him and turn from evil. He intended for the brief scriptural mentions of evil to be enough to keep us from it. The other ancient texts quoted here are simply further evidence that man once knew the truth and still had fragments of it in his memories, even as he wrote his own ideas and imaginings and invented his own religions.

1. Marriage: the divine relationship

While the entire material creation was still very good, before sin entered the material universe, Adam established the first marriage, and laid the groundwork for all future marriages. Jesus quoted Adam's "wedding vows" when He condemned divorce, giving this statement the authority of God.

> *And He answered and said to them, 'Have you not read that He who made them at the beginning made them male and female, and said, "For this cause a man shall leave father and mother and shall cling to his wife, and the two of them shall be one flesh? Therefore they are no longer two, but one flesh. Therefore what God has joined together, let not man separate."'* (Matthew 19:4-6 NASB)

Removed skillfully and carefully, certain rib tissue will regenerate,[4] even today. God made Eve to be one with Adam, and Adam understood that it went beyond just the physical fact that she was created from part of him.

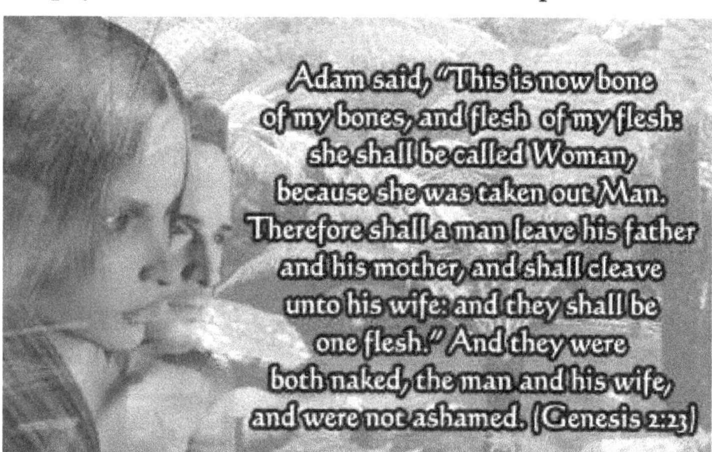

"And Adam said, This is now bone of my bones, and flesh of my flesh: she shall be called Woman, because she was taken out of Man. Therefore shall a man leave his father and his mother, and shall cleave unto his wife: and they shall be one flesh. And they were both naked, the man and his wife, and were not ashamed."
Genesis 2: 23-25

2. Marriage: one flesh

> *The man said, "This is now bone of my bones, And flesh of my flesh; She shall be called Woman, Because she was taken out of Man." For this reason a man shall leave his father and his mother, and be joined to his wife; and they shall become one flesh. And the man and his wife were both naked and were not ashamed.* Genesis 2: 23-25 NASB

The standard Adam gave to the human race, and to all his children forever, is marriage. Two people through sexual intercourse become one flesh. The concept of one flesh is ridiculed by Secular Humanists today, and Satan attacked marriage from the beginning. Satan knew that his greatest chance for success in making man fall was to use Eve to tempt Adam. Satan believed that once he succeeded in deceiving Eve, Adam would eat the fruit to avoid being separated from her. This tactic is so well known that it is a common motif through much of the world's literature.

Cassandra painting by Evelyn De Morgan (1885-1919) US Public Domain

3. Corrupting the human race by corrupting marriage

One corruption of the serpent's promise to give special knowledge to a woman is found in Greek mythology. Cassandra was the daughter of King Priam and Queen Hecuba of Troy. One version of this story says that she spent a night at Apollo's temple, at which time the temple snakes licked her ears clean so that she was able to hear the future. This myth, rightly interpreted, makes Apollo a picture of Satan, since he seduced Cassandra with the temptation of secret knowledge but planned to corrupt her by demanding sex, and cursed her with her prophecies not being believed because she refused him.[5]

E. Why Was the Tree In the Garden?

Compared to the question "Why did God create Satan?", this has an easy answer. God's original creation was very good. This included the Tree of the Knowledge of Good and Evil. We are also told that the garden which God placed in Eden was for man. Very simple logic tells us that the very good Tree of the Knowledge of Good and Evil was for Adam and Eve, or perhaps their children. They just were not ready for it yet. Just as we do not want a five-year-old driving a car or piloting a plane, so Adam and Eve were not yet ready for the tree of the Knowledge of Good and Evil. Just because a five-year-old driver would probably wreck anything he attempted to drive or fly does not mean that we should not have any cars or airplanes.

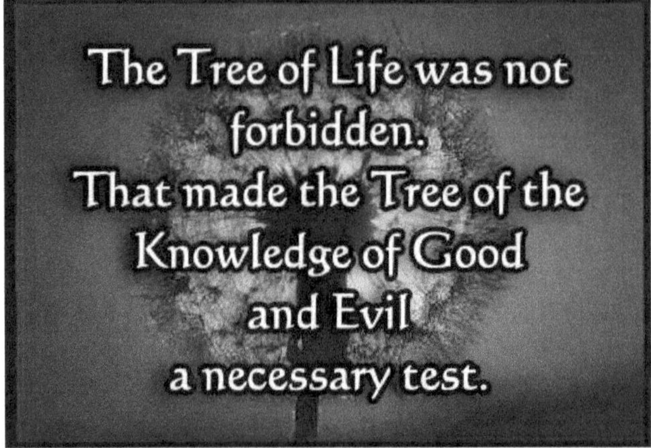

The Tree of Life was not forbidden. That made the Tree of the Knowledge of Good and Evil a necessary test.

God was developing moral character. So sin is deliberate disobedience to God. That is why the first of the Ten Commandments is *Thou shalt have no other gods before me.* (Exodus 20:3) That is the negative of what Jesus said is the first and great commandment: *Thou shalt love the LORD thy God with all thine heart, and with all thy soul, and with all thy might.* (Deuteronomy 6:5, Matthew 22:37, Mark 12:30, Luke 10:27).

We are told that sin is "fun." The enjoyment of rebellion is temporary. As Moses understood, *Choosing rather to suffer affliction with the people of God, than to enjoy the pleasures of sin for a season;* (Hebrews 11:25, KJV) The fun of sin is usually very short-lived, only a few hours. *The pleasures of sin* might last a lifetime, but there is no pleasure in sin beyond the grave.

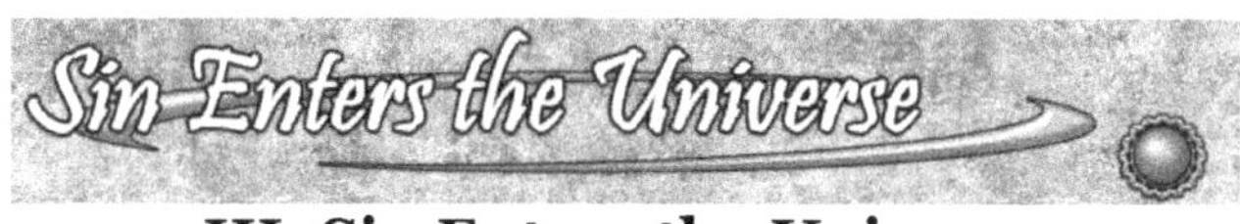

III. Sin Enters the Universe

A. The Fall

The Fall defines the human race and the entire material universe. Yet Genesis describes it in one chapter of twenty-four average-length verses. We can examine alternate meanings for words and phrases. We can examine the opinions of others, especially ancient sources. But as Solomon said three thousand years ago, *there is nothing new under the sun.*

1. The temptation

At the end of God's creative process, God "planted a garden eastward in Eden." Though it was made especially for man, many creatures besides Adam and Eve lived in that garden. One of them was the serpent.

Now the serpent was more subtle than any beast of the field which the LORD God had made. Genesis 3:1a KJV

Now the Nachash was more arum (cunning, crafty, wily) than any beast of the sadeh which Hashem Elohim had made. (Genesis 3:1 *Orthodox Jewish Bible*)[6] (transliterations instead of translations for some words multiple meanings in English; English letters for the actual Hebrew letters)

Now the Shining One was more clever than any animal of the field that the LORD God had made. (Genesis 3:1 ISV)

Subtle means crafty, sneaky, clever at doing things you really should not be doing. The same word is used in other places in a good sense to mean prudent or sensible.

Every prudent man acts with knowledge, But a fool displays folly. Proverbs 13:6 NASB

Subtle is the defining characteristic of the serpent. From the very beginning different types of animals had different characteristics. The nature of a sheep is to be part of the herd, naïve, in need of a shepherd. Hawks are solitary birds of prey. Foxes, crows, wolves, crocodiles and other creatures are known to be crafty, subtle. The serpent was subtler than any of these. But this is not one of Aesop's fables or just an allegory. This is an historical record.

As an historical record of actual events, several questions must be answered.

a. How could the serpent decide to do evil?

How could a creature which God created *very good* decide to do evil? While there is no clear answer in the Word of God, animals, like humans, have the ability to choose, to make decisions. The most likely answer seems to be, at least to us, that the serpent chose, or at least was deceived, as was Eve, into allowing Satan to use it. There is no final answer to this question.

b. Was it a snake or a dinosaur?

Dinosaur in a Las Vegas Museum photo by Tammy Sue http://www.publicdomain pictures.net/

Was the creature what we today call a snake, or might it have been what we call a dinosaur? Part of the curse made the serpent *"cursed above all cattle, and above every beast of the field; upon thy belly shalt thou go, and dust shalt thou eat all the days of thy life"* (Genesis 3:14). This clearly says that as part of the curse, the serpent changed form. All snakes which crawl on their bellies are genetic descendants of this serpent. Satan is called both a serpent and a dragon. This fact convinced many that the original serpent was a dragon, a creature with legs and wings. Since God's original creation included many individual animals of the same kind, it seems that the creatures we know as snakes all come from this serpent. The rest of this "kind" of creature did not change form at this time. They might be what we know as lizards, perhaps even dinosaurs (dragons).

The Bible contains many references to various kinds of reptiles, so it is possible to at least form theories about the nature of the serpent in the garden. It mentions serpents, lizards, creatures that might have been dinosaurs, and even refers to dragons.

c. Was the ability of an animal to talk unusual?

Since the serpent carried on a conversation, first with Eve, then with the LORD, was this something unusual, even a miracle, or was this common? The fact that the serpent could speak, however, is a subject about which the Bible says very little. There is only one other instance in the Bible of an animal speaking.

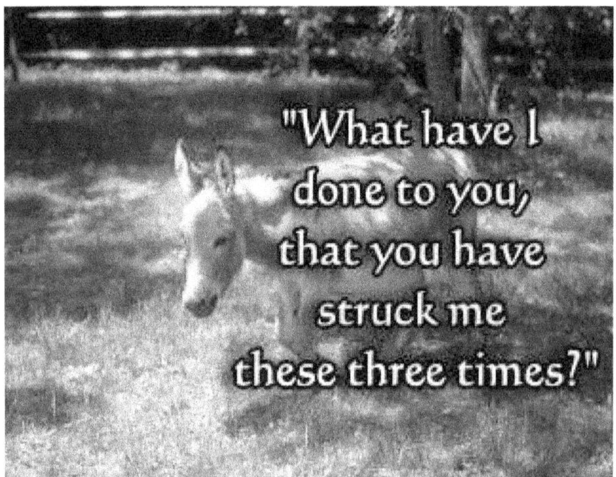

Donkey image with the question asked by Balaam 's donkey from thepassage below. Image in the public domain

And the LORD opened the mouth of the donkey, and she said to Balaam, "What have I done to you, that you have struck me these three times?" Then Balaam said to the donkey, "Because you have made a mockery of me! If there had been a sword in my hand, I would

> *have killed you by now." The donkey said to Balaam, "Am I not your donkey on which you have ridden all your life to this day? Have I ever been accustomed to do so to you?" And he said, "No."* (Numbers 22:28-30)

Balaam's donkey speaking to him is the only other time an animal talks in the Bible. Because animals do not talk today, unbelievers label both of these events fables or allegories. These two instances are not fables or allegories. Nor are these like modern animals, such as parrots and myna birds, mimicking human speech without understanding. They are historical events of animals both using human speech with understanding on both sides of the conversation. In the case of Balaam, the record clearly states that the LORD opened the mouth of the donkey. Neither Balaam nor anyone with him expected a donkey to talk. This was highly unusual. Yet Balaam does not react with fright. Balaam talks to and eventually even listens to the donkey.

Josephus said that before the fall "… all the living creatures had one language."[7] The concept that all the animals talked before the fall is supported by Philo and the books of *Jasher* and *Jubilees*. It seems to be supported by all of the most ancient sources.

Yet our research is unable to find any support for animals talking in any Jewish commentary: not any Talmud, Midrash, or any Sedar. The nearly unanimous Jewish position for around two thousand years is that the Serpent was empowered by Lucifer and Balaam's donkey was empowered by God. The only times they ever spoke or were able to speak were the two occasions mentioned in the Scriptures.

This does not exclude God or demons empowering animals to speak on some other occasion not included in the Word of God. But it does exclude a time when animals talked before the Fall.

d. Was the serpent used or possessed by Satan?

Most important, was the serpent used by Satan the way demons took over human bodies during the New Testament time period, or was the serpent actually Satan?

Today, horse trainers work to break a horse's will but not its spirit. All animals, not just horses, have a will. The individual serpent that talked to Eve had a will. Though God has not chosen to reveal all that we would like to know about this incident, there is a possible New Testament parallel.

Horse jumping photo by Edward McCabe http://www.publicdomain pictures.net/

When Jesus cast the "legion" of demons out of the Gerasene man, he allowed this large number of demons to enter, to "possess" (or at least attempt to possess, considering the outcome), a herd of pigs. Based on this evidence, it seems to be most reasonable to assume that Satan, created as a spiritual, non-material being, possessed the serpent in the same way the New Testament records demon possessions of humans or animals.

Satan seems to have used the will of the serpent as a horse trainer uses the will of the horse. Because God judged the serpent, it seems that the serpent had both intellect and volition. The serpent permitted itself to be used by Satan.

Some argue that Satan was originally created both as a serpent (dinosaur?/dragon?) as well as the anointed cherub that covers. If this is true, this would make the original Satan to be the original serpent. This might be true, but we have no information to back that argument up. We know that all of the animals of the original creation have died and that Satan, as a spiritual being, still exists.

2. What Is Sin?

According to Josephus, Eve was used to talking to all the animals. "... All the living creatures had one language, at that time the serpent, which then lived together with Adam and his wife, shewed an envious disposition ..."[8] So according to Josephus, the serpent was the first material creature to sin.

a. Sin Begins With Desire.

> *The serpent said to the woman, "Indeed, has God said, 'You shall not eat from any tree of the garden'?" The woman said to the serpent, "From the fruit of the trees of the garden we may eat; but from the fruit of the tree which is in the middle of the garden, God has said, 'You shall not eat from it or touch it, or you will die.'" The serpent said to the woman, "You surely will not die! For God knows that in the day you eat from it your eyes will be opened, and you will be like God, knowing good and evil."* (Genesis 3:1b-4, NASB)

And he (the serpent) *said unto the woman, Yea hath God said, Ye shall not eat of every tree of the garden?*

(Genesis 3:1b) In what we call civilized societies, we categorize evil. First degree (premeditated) murder is the worst. Sexual assault, assault and battery, grand theft, arson, and kidnapping are nearly as bad, and sometimes carry worse punishments, depending on things such as intent and the degree of harm.

b. Sin Is a Choice.

This question of the serpent would be under the category today of a "little white lie." Not so bad by the standards of "civilized society." Eve might have felt a little uneasy, but maybe not. She did not cry out for help. With just the first question, she might not have even understood that what the serpent said was wrong. After the serpent created a desire in Eve for something forbidden, the Tree of Knowledge, He tempted her to choose to sin, and thereby tempted Adam by forcing a choice on Adam.

c. Sin Is Disobedience and Rebellion.

When the woman saw that the tree was good for food, and that it was a delight to the eyes, and that the tree was desirable to make one wise, she took from its fruit and ate; and she gave also to her husband with her, and he ate. Genesis 3:6 NASB

Adam was not deceived, but the woman being deceived was in the transgression. 1 Timothy 2:14 NASB

d. Sin Has Consequences.

Ussher, in his *Annals of the World,* describes the Fall, and the future hope contained in the pronouncements of God. It is important to remember that the promised Redeemer is present here as much as sin and evil are present.

> He [Satan] tempted the woman to sin by the serpent. By this he got the name and title of the old serpent. Re 12:9 20:2 The woman was beguiled by the serpent and the man seduced by

> the woman. They broke the command of God concerning the forbidden fruit. Accordingly when sought for by God and convicted of this crime, each had their punishments imposed on them. *This promise was also given that the seed of the woman should one day break the serpent's head. Christ, in the fullness of time should undo the works of the Devil.* 1 John 3:8 Romans 16:20 Adam first called her Eve because she was then ordained to be the mother, not only of all that should live this natural life, *but, of those also who should live by faith in her seed.*[9]

e. Sin Causes Shame.

Just after Creation, before the Fall, God records an observation about Adam and Eve that, to a twenty-first century westerner, seems to be the strangest statement to show the distinction between man in his state of innocence and after the fall of the human race.

And they were both naked, the man and his wife, and were not ashamed. Genesis 2:25

There was no one else, so how could there be shame? Shame is defined as confusion caused by disappointment. It is the embarrassment of dishonor. There is no possible embarrassment, dishonor, disappointment, or any other type of shame between a husband and wife. Of course there was no shame before the fall. How could there be? Why does God say this?

The "Adam and Eve Tablet" includes a man and a woman seated on either side of a tree, with a serpent also present in the image. Figures are clothed but the setting still resembles the Garden of Eden in Genesis Public Domain Image British Museum Collection

These questions are found in every ancient culture. One very clear example is the "Adam and Eve Tablet"[10] pictured above. It includes a man and a woman seated on either side of a tree, with a serpent also present in the image. These figures are clothed but the setting still resembles the Garden in Genesis. Some sources speak of

Adam and Eve being "clothed in innocence" or in God's righteousness, before the fall and this tablet may actually attempt to depict that state. Since Secular Humanist cannot allow the smallest seed of truth, they added the following disclaimer. This disclaimer, quoted below, is now included in the description at the British Museum exhibit.

> "Originally thought to be a depiction of the Biblical Adam and Eve tempted by the serpent, it achieved remarkable notoriety in Britain during the 19th century as the 'Adam and Eve Seal' or 'Temptation Seal' and was popularly viewed as validation of biblical accounts. A century later, museum scholars determined it to be one of a well-known class of mythic scenarios featuring one of the earliest historical images of the Tree Of Life, timeless Mesopotamian symbol of earthly creation."

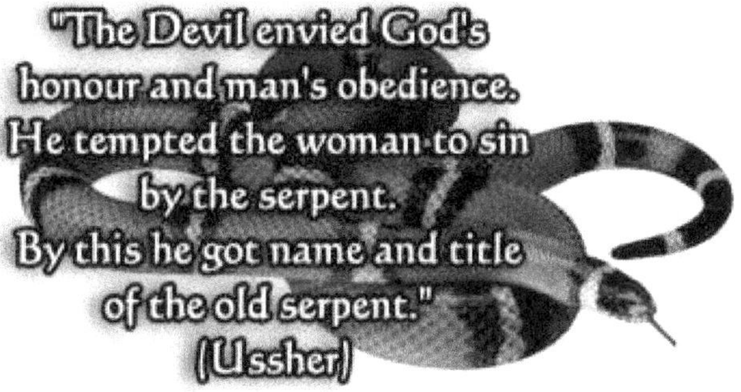

Snake image. The Devil envied God's honour and man's obedience. He tempted the woman to sin by the serpent. By this he got his name and title of the old serpent." Ussher

"God therefore commanded that Adam and his wife should eat of all the rest of the plants, but to abstain from the Tree of Knowledge; and foretold to them, that if they touched it, it would prove their destruction. But while all the living creatures had one language, at that time the serpent, which then lived together with Adam and his wife, shewed an envious disposition, at his supposal of their living happily, and in obedience to the commands of God; and imagining, that when they disobeyed them, they would fall into calamities, he persuaded the woman, out of a malicious intention, to taste of the tree of knowledge of good and evil; which knowledge, when they should obtain, they would lead a happy life; nay, a life not inferior to that of a god: by which means he overcame the woman, and persuaded her to despise the command of God."[11] (Josephus)

3. The Lie

The serpent had to eventually abandon half-truths, "little white lies" and "tell a whopper."

And the serpent said unto the woman, *"Ye shall not surely die: For God doth know that in the day ye eat thereof, then your eyes shall opened, and ye shall be as gods, knowing good and evil."* (Genesis 3:4,5)

Shakespeare put these words in Mercutio's mouth after he was stabbed in a swordfight: "No, 'tis not so deep as a well, nor so wide as a church-door; but 'tis enough, 'twill serve: ask for me to-morrow, and you shall find me a grave man."[12] Though Mercutio could still talk, like Adam and Eve, he knew that his wound was fatal. Mercutio knew that he would be in the grave tomorrow.

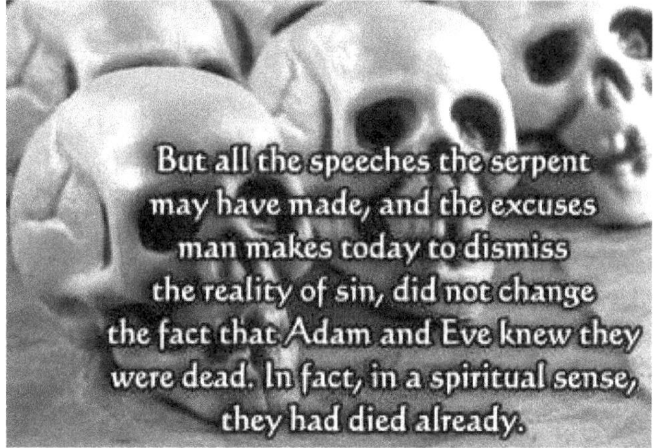

Public domain image of skulls. "But all the speeches the serpent made, and all the excuses man makes today to dismiss the reality of sin, did not change the fact that Adam and Eve knew they were dead. In fact, in a spiritual sense, they had died already."

> *And when the woman saw that the tree was good for food, and that it was pleasant to the eyes, and a tree to be desired to make one wise, she took of the fruit thereof, and did eat, and gave also unto her husband with her; and he did eat. And the eyes of them both were opened, and they knew that they were naked; and they sewed fig leaves together, and made themselves aprons.* (Genesis 3:6,7)

Eve was deceived. Adam chose his wife above the Word of God and rebelled. God never wanted Adam and Eve to experience evil. He desired only that they know Him and enjoy Him forever. God wanted them, as He wants us, to fully and intimately know and experience good without the knowledge and experience of evil. Instead of the promised freedom, they had knowledge of the bondage of death.

4. The Results of the Fall

For the human race, the material world, and everything we know as the universe, sin and the curse began with Adam.

a. Shame

And the eyes of them both were opened, and they knew that they were naked; and they sewed fig leaves together, and made themselves aprons. And they heard the voice of the Lord God walking in the garden in the cool of the day: and Adam and his wife hid themselves from the presence of the Lord God amongst the trees of the garden. (Genesis 3:7,8)

b. Fear

And the Lord God called unto Adam, and said unto him, Where art thou? And he said, I heard thy voice in the garden, and I was afraid, because I was naked; and I hid myself. (Genesis 3:9,10)

c. Accountability

And he said, Who told thee that thou wast naked? Hast thou eaten of the tree, whereof I commanded thee that thou shouldest not eat? And the man said, The woman whom thou gavest to be with me, she gave me of the tree, and I did eat. (Genesis 3:11,12)

d. Responsibility

Then the Lord God said to the woman, "What is this you have done?" And the woman said, "The serpent deceived me, and I ate." (Genesis 3:13 NASB)

e. The Curse

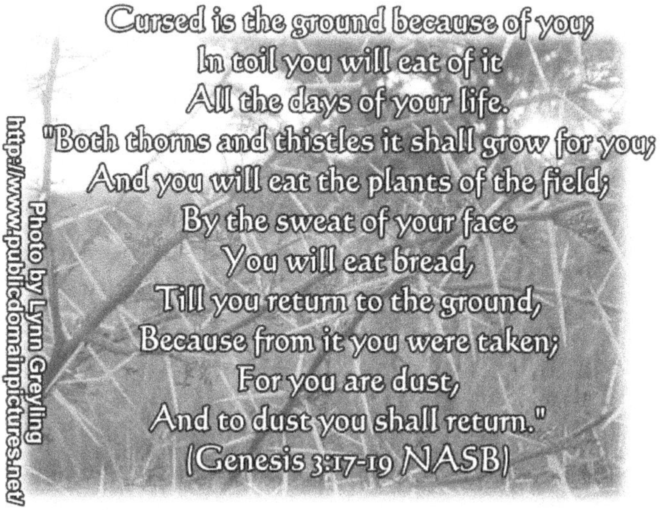

Then to Adam He said, "Because you have listened to the voice of your wife, and have eaten from the tree about which I commanded you, saying, 'You shall not eat from it'; cursed is the ground because of you; in toil you will eat of it all the days of your life. Both thorns and thistles it shall grow for you; And you will eat the plants of the field; By the sweat of your face you will eat bread, till you return to the ground, Because from it you were taken; for you are dust,and to dust you shall return." (Genesis 3: 17-19 NASB)

For we know that the whole creation groans and suffers the pains of childbirth together until now. (Romans 8:22, NASB)

And we know that we are of God, and the whole world lieth in wickedness. (I John 6:19)

f. Death

Surely, I was brought forth in avon; and in chet did immi conceive me[13] [i.e., I was a sinner from conception]. (Psalm 51:5 [7] Orthodox Jewish Bible) [Note that some versions have different verse numberings, which is why this reference includes both verse 5 and verse 7.]

Wherefore, as by one man sin entered into the world, and death by sin; and so death passed upon all men, for that all have sinned. (Romans 5:12)

The physical evidences of sin: death, disease, and the curse, are everywhere. It is not necessary to examine as many other ancient writings in this work, in contrast to *COA Part One: The Scientific History of Origins.*

The entire material universe is under the curse of sin. Sometime in the future God's atonement will remove that curse.

> *"For just as the new heavens and the new earth Which I make will endure before Me," declares the Lord, "So your offspring and your name will endure.* (Isaiah 66:22 NASB)
>
> *Then I saw a new heaven and a new earth; for the first heaven and the first earth passed away, and there is no longer any sea.* (Revelation 21:1)
>
> *And there shall be no more curse: but the throne of God and of the Lamb shall be in it; and his servants shall serve him:* (Revelation 22:3)

B. The Knowledge of Good and Evil

Adam and Eve now had the knowledge of good and evil. And the eyes of them both were opened. Nothing externally changed with them, yet they understood that they were naked. "So what?" They were naked before they ate the fruit and they were still naked. There were no other humans to see their nakedness. Except perhaps for the serpent, the animals did not care. The Lord God had created them and understood them intimately. So why was their first reaction to make aprons of fig leaves? There in the garden, what was wrong with being naked?

This is the foundation to understanding the entire human race and the entire Word of God. Even Atheists understand this. If there was no sin causing a Fall and the Universe is not under a curse, there is no need for an atonement, no need for a sinless Savior, no need for the Law or the resurrection. Liberals who claim that this is some type of "allegory" are denying the entire Word of God. To a liberal, the time and detail we spend on this one event in the historic record might seem unnecessary. Jesus does not believe that understanding the cause of sin is unnecessary.

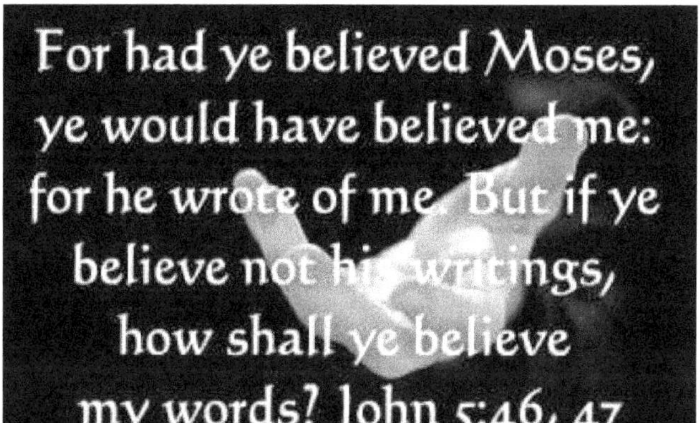

"For had ye believed Moses, ye would have believed me; for he wrote of me. But if ye believe not his writings, how shall ye believe my words?" (John 5:46,47)

1. Their Understanding Was Sharpened.

On this key, important, foundational doctrine, the New International Translation not only incorrectly translates Genesis 2:25 but destroys the Word of God in process.

Adam and his wife were both naked, and they ***felt no shame***. NIV

The Scriptures do not say, they *felt* they were naked, but that they *knew* they were naked. Though they certainly felt shame, the important fact was not the change in the way they felt. Rather it was a change in their understanding. Josephus is not inspired. In certain sections he has many errors, such as equating the Hyksos with the Children of Israel in slavery in Egypt. But his insight in this passage clarifies the fall.

> *"Upon this they perceived that they were become naked to one another; and being ashamed thus to appear abroad, they invented somewhat to cover them;* ***for the tree sharpened their understanding;*** *and they covered themselves with fig-leaves; and tying these before them, out of modesty, they thought they were happier than they were before, as they had discovered what they were in want of."*[14] (Josephus)

A very important point in understanding this passage is not easily translated into English. The Orthodox Jewish Bible contains a number of transliterations of critical words.

> *And they were both* ***arummim*** *(naked ones), the adam and his isha [woman, wife], and were not ashamed. Now the Nachash [Serpent] was more* ***arum*** *(cunning, crafty, wiley) than any beast of the sadeh ... And the eyes of them both were opened, and they knew that they were* ***eirummim*** *(naked ones);* (Bereshis 2:25-3:1& 7)[15]

> *Now the man and his wife were both naked (nude) and were not ashamed. ... Now the serpent was more crafty (shrewd) than any*

> *beast of the field ...Then the eyes of both of them were opened, and they knew that they were naked; (nude)* (*Genesis 2:25-3:1 & 7* NASB)

The addition of the words "nude" and "shrewd" emphasize that in Hebrew this is the same word in all three places. In the LXX (Septuagint) they are different words, so we know that the English translations are correct for meaning. The LXX and the various translations have the correct meaning, but they miss the important Hebrew word play. The serpent was also naked (*nude*) and Adam and Eve were also crafty (*shrewd*). The serpent was crafty in the sense of *candid.* We use the words "naked" or "candid" the same way today, as in "the naked truth," meaning complete and unembellished. *Now the serpent was more naked* (secondary meaning) than any beast of the field. Apparently the serpent was known for speaking his mind, for being open and candid. Yet what he told Eve, though designed to sound honest and truthful, was completely dishonest. This word play also explains the embarrassment of Adam and Eve. They understood that they were tricked, deceived, and were humiliated.

English poetry uses rhymes to encourage comparisons and convey relationships in meanings. This is illustrated in the above use of "nude" and "shrewd." To a lesser extent it uses *homophones,* words that sound alike but have different meanings, such as "the man rode down the road". In the *Romeo and Juliet* example above, "a grave man," the word "grave" meaning both "serious" as in *seriously injured,* and "dead" or *in a grave*. Hebrew poetry relies much more heavily on wordplays and homophones and the original Hebrew words are a strong example of that.

Another Scripture passage gives insight into Adam and Eve's state of mind after the fall, explaining the truth about their new knowledge. Hebrews 10:33 discusses the implications of being exposed and humiliated. The International Standard Bible Encyclopedia's commentary clarifies how this applies to Adam and Eve's *"knowledge of good and evil"*.

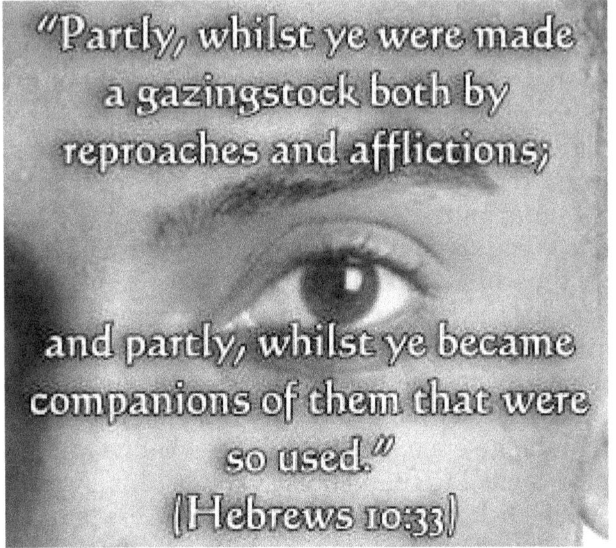

"Partly, whilst ye were made a gazingstock both by reproaches and afflictions; and partly, whilst ye became companions of them that were so used." (Hebrews 10:33)

> "In Hebrews 10:33, 'gazingstock' is the translation of *theatrizo,* 'to bring upon the theater,' 'to be made a spectacle of,' 'made a gazing stock both by reproaches and afflictions'; compare 1 Corinthians 4:9, *theatron ginomai,* where Paul says the apostles were *'made a spectacle unto the world,'* the King James Version margin '(Greek) theater.' The reference in both instances is to the custom of exhibiting criminals, and especially gladiators, men doomed to death, in theaters. 'In the morning

> men are exposed to lions and bears; at mid-day to their spectators; those that kill are exposed to one another; the victor is detained for another slaughter; the conclusion of the fight is death.' We are apt to forget what the first preachers and professors of Christianity had to endure."[16]

Adam and Eve were therefore made aware that they were exposed, nude, to the entire spiritual world. Possibly spiritual beings, such as angels, had been observing them all along, and those in rebellion with Satan were already jealous of their relationship with God and lustful over them, watching them the way wild beasts and gladiators in the arena sized up their future prey or opponents.

2. Their Eyes Were Opened.

The traditional position of the Church is that the actual fruit was unimportant. It was the act of rebellion which caused the Fall. Though this is certainly true, that the Fall was caused by the act of rebellion, I no longer believe that the fruit itself was unimportant.

Graham Hancock, in his book *Supernatural: Meetings with the Ancient Teachers of Mankind*, believes that the fruit Adam and Eve ate "sharpened their understanding" (as referred to earlier, in the quote from Josephus) through a psychotropic effect.[17] In some way it gave them what we would call a "high" that opened doors to spiritual understanding.

Eating the fruit allowed them to "see" things that our material eyes cannot see, such as angels with them in the garden. Correctly seeing and interpreting these spiritual visions required personal discipline and great maturity. Adam and Eve simply did not yet have these at that time. They would have become ready for the fruit in the future, but were not ready yet.

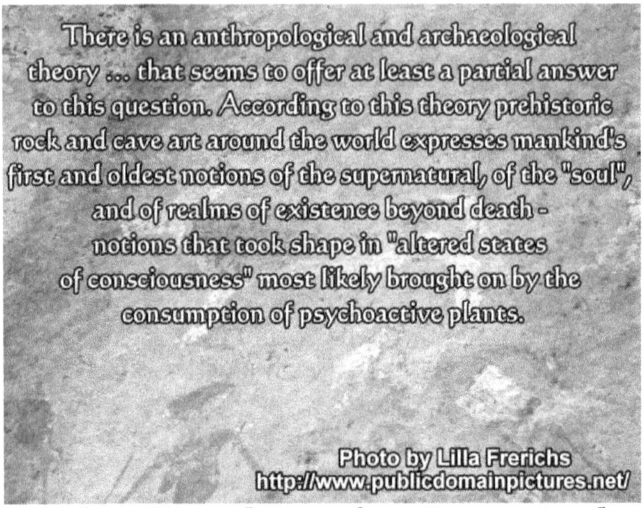

Graham Hancock quote from *Supernatural: Meetings with the Ancient Teachers of Mankind*: "There is an anthropological and archaeological theory ... that seems to offer at least a partial answer to this question. According to this theory prehistoric rock and cave art around the world expresses mankind's first and oldest notions of the supernatural, of the "soul," and of realms of existence beyond death -- notions that took shape in 'altered states of consciousness' most likely brought on by the consumption of psychoactive plants." Photo by Lilla Frerichs http://www.publicdomainpictures.net/

a. Elisha

There are several people who had their “eyes opened” in this way throughout the Word of God. In 2 Kings 6, Elisha the prophet faces capture by the King of Syria for informing Ahab of his plans of ambush and attack before they happen. This passage does not involve an outside agent like the forbidden fruit but still is an example of the spiritual insight made possible by having one’s eyes opened. The important part of Elisha’s servant having his eyes opened was the complete change in his attitude when he understood the reality of his situation. Unlike

Adam and Eve, this occasion of having his eyes opened was great comfort.

> *And when the servant of the man of God was risen early, and gone forth, behold, an host compassed the city both with horses and chariots. And his servant said unto him, Alas, my master! how shall we do?*
> *And he answered, Fear not: for they that be with us are more than they that be with them.*

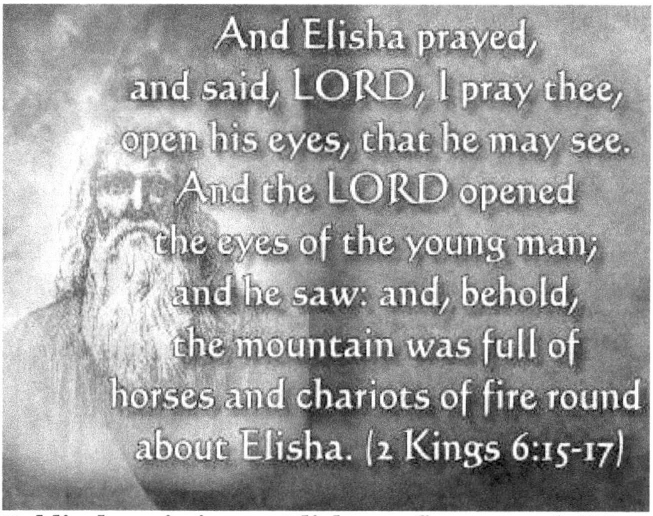

Public domain image Elisha on fire ground. "Now when the attendant of the man of God had risen early and gone out, behold, an army with horses and chariots was circling the city. And his servant said to him, "Alas, my master! What shall we do?" So he answered, "Do not fear, for those who are with us are more than those who are with them." Then Elisha prayed and said, "O Lord, I pray, open his eyes that he may see." And the Lord opened the servant's eyes and he saw; and behold, the mountain was full of horses and chariots of fire all around Elisha. (2 Kings 6: 15-17)

When the servant of the man of God had his eyes opened, like Adam and Eve had their eyes opened, he clearly saw that there were more beings for them than the army against them. It caused the servant of God to rejoice, realizing that the man of God would triumph over God's enemies.

b. Balaam

But Balaam, the man *"whose eyes are open,"* used that understanding to rebel against the LORD. He was a servant of God. He spoke with God and God gave him insight. At the beginning of his story in Numbers 22:18, he makes this statement:

"Though Balak were to give me his house full of silver and gold, I could not do anything, either small or great, contrary to the command of the Lord my God." (NASB)

When Balaam arrives in Moab, he begins by claiming while in a trance that his eyes are open. The KJV is the best translation for the meaning, sense, or intent of the passage. However, some might point out that a literal word-for-word translation is very different. While that is true, it does not alter the meaning of the passage. In this case, a more literal translation says that Balaam's physical eyes were closed (v 3) in order to open his eyes to the message God had for him.

> *And he took up his parable, and said, Balaam the son of Beor hath said, and the man whose eyes are open hath said: He hath said, which heard the words of God, which saw the vision of the Almighty, falling into a trance, but having his eyes open:* (Numbers 24:3,4)
>
> *And he took up his parable, and said, Balaam the son of Beor hath said, and the man whose eyes are open hath said: He hath said, which heard the words of God, and knew the knowledge of the most High, which saw the vision of the Almighty, falling into a trance, but having his eyes open:* (Numbers 24:15, NASB)

We don't know if it was part of Balaam's insight, his "opened eyes", that allowed him to speak to and understand his donkey. The Scriptures say, as mentioned before, that God opened the donkey's mouth. They also say that Balaam's prophecies blessing Israel came to him as a result of God having *"put a word in Balaam's mouth."* We also know that Balaam's insight failed him when it came to seeing the angel of God sent with a sword to express God's anger.

> *Then the Lord opened the eyes of Balaam, and he saw the angel of the Lord standing in the way with his drawn sword in his hand; and he bowed all the way to the ground. The angel of the Lord said to him, "Why have you struck your donkey these three times? Behold, I have come out as an adversary, because your way was contrary to me. But the donkey saw me and turned aside from me these three times. If she had not turned aside from me, I would surely have killed you just now, and let her live." Balaam said to the angel of the Lord, "I have sinned, for I did not know that you were standing in the way against me. Now then, if it is displeasing to you, I will turn back." But the angel of the Lord said to Balaam, "Go with the men, but you shall speak only the word which I tell you." So Balaam went along with the leaders of Balak.* (Numbers 22:31-35)

Balaam clearly acknowledges that it was his sin that prevented him from seeing the angel. Balaam had his understanding sharpened, which allowed him to prophesy correctly, but his opened eyes did not prevent him from rebelling against the Lord. And this rebellion cost him his life.

Numbers 31:8 records Balaam's fate.

> *"They killed the kings of Midian along with the rest of their slain: Evi and Rekem and Zur and Hur and Reba, the five kings of Midian; they also killed Balaam the son of Beor with the sword."* (NASB)

The question of why he was killed is answered in Revelation 2:14.

Public domain image of a brass urn on a landscape background. "But I have a few things against you, because you have there some who hold the teaching of Balaam, who kept teaching Balak to put a stumbling block before the sons of Israel, to eat things sacrificed to idols and to commit acts of immorality."

c. Divination Condemned in the Law

Josephus was clearly correct that **"the tree sharpened their understanding."** The "opened eyes" are also referred to in the Word of God as a "gateway." The rebels after the flood attempted to build a "gateway" to the spiritual realm by building a tower at Babel (possible meaning: Bab (gate)-el (god); a gateway to god). God Himself judged this attempt.

All attempts by men to communicate directly with the Spiritual world are condemned in the Law.

> *When thou art come into the land which the LORD thy God giveth thee, thou shalt not learn to do after the abominations of those nations. There shall not be found among you any one that maketh his son or his daughter to pass through the fire, or that useth divination, or an observer of times, or an enchanter, or a witch, or a charmer, or a consulter with familiar spirits, or a wizard, or a necromancer. For all that do these things are an abomination unto the LORD: and because of these abominations the LORD thy God doth drive them out from before thee. Thou shalt be perfect with the LORD thy God. For these nations, which thou shalt possess, hearkened unto observers of times, and unto diviners: but as for thee, the LORD thy God hath not suffered thee so to do.* (Deuteronomy 18:9-14)

One possible translation of Genesis 2:15 ISV has Adam responsible for guarding the Garden of Eden.

The LORD God took the man and placed him in the Garden of Eden in order to have him work it and guard it.

Since this is a legitimate translation, the question arises; What was he guarding it from? Everything God had created on earth was, to this point either good or very good. The only possible answer is evil from outside the material universe.

If this interpretation is correct, then the evil Adam was to guard against is the same evil Moses warns us against here in this section of the Law.

> *Anyone who sacrifices his son or daughter in fire, practices divination, interprets omens, practices sorcery, casts spells, or who is a medium, an occultist, or a necromancer.* (Deuteronomy 18:10,11 ISV)

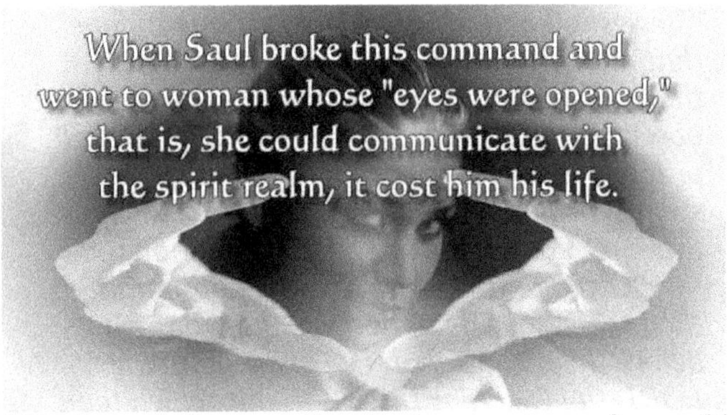

Public domain image of a shadowy woman framed by hands. When Saul broke this command and went to a woman whose “eyes wre opened,” that is, she could communicate with the spirit realm, it cost him his life.

d. Saul

> *And Saul disguised himself, and put on other raiment, and he went, and two men with him, and they came to the woman by night: and he said, I pray thee, divine unto me by the familiar spirit, and bring me him up, whom I shall name unto thee. Then said the woman, Whom shall I bring up unto thee? And he said, Bring me up Samuel. And when the woman saw Samuel, she cried with a loud voice: and the woman spake to Saul, saying, Why hast thou deceived me? for thou art Saul. And the*

> *king said unto her, Be not afraid: for what sawest thou? And the woman said unto Saul, I saw gods ascending out of the earth. And he said unto her, What form is he of? And she said, An old man cometh up; and he is covered with a mantle. And Saul perceived that it was Samuel, and he stooped with his face to the ground, and bowed himself.* (1 Samuel 28: 8,11-14)

The woman brought up the spirit of Samuel from the dead by divination. When her "eyes were opened" she knew who Saul was, immediately seeing through his disguise. She saw spiritual beings and called them "gods." We know that one of these beings was not a god, but Samuel.

Secularists at this point might say that God was cruel or unfair. He had refused to answer Saul in the ways that were "accepted". When Saul became desperate and used a forbidden means to get an answer, God gave him an answer, but also condemned him for doing "the only thing that worked". Believers might despair of pleasing God and successfully doing right. But remember, God created everything "very good." Even divination can be carried out in the right way and be successful.

e. Daniel

> *Daniel answered in the presence of the king, and said, The secret which the king hath demanded cannot the wise men, the astrologers, the magicians, the soothsayers, shew unto the king; But there is a God in heaven that revealeth secrets, and maketh known to the king Nebuchadnezzar what shall be in the latter days. Thy dream, and the visions of thy head upon thy bed, are these; As for thee, O king, thy thoughts came into thy mind upon thy bed, what should come to pass*

> *hereafter: and he that revealeth secrets maketh known to thee what shall come to pass. But as for me, this secret is not revealed to me for any wisdom that I have more than any living, but for their sakes that shall make known the interpretation to the king, and that thou mightest know the thoughts of thy heart.* (Daniel 2:27-30)

f. Joseph

And Pharaoh said unto Joseph, I have dreamed a dream, and there is none that can interpret it: and I have heard say of thee, that thou canst understand a dream to interpret it. 16 And Joseph answered Pharaoh, saying, It is not in me: God shall give Pharaoh an answer of peace. (Genesis 41:15,16)

g. Ezekiel

Ezekiel began his vision with the words *"the heavens were opened, and I saw visions of God... As I looked, and behold, a whirlwind came out of the north..."* (Ezekiel 1:1,4) In language very similar to Genesis, Ezekiel's eyes were opened, not in sinful rebellion, but by God.

h. John

But the most complete opening of the understanding was the Apostle John. Those whose hearts are darkened, who are spiritually dead and have their eyes blinded, do not understand this vision. They mock, calling this vision "some sort of wild LSD trip."

i. Enoch

The Book of Enoch[18] is not considered inspired, but it is believed to have been written in ancient times. It speaks about spiritual beings who observed Heaven and also Earth, and could look at God's and man's activities. It also hints at what may have been Satan's original rebellion.

Public domain image of a fragment from the Book of Enoch

> **From Chapter 2**
> 1. "All who are in the heavens know what is transacted there ... without transgressing the commands, which they have received."
> 2. "They behold the earth, and understand what is there transacted, from the beginning to the end of it."
> **From Chapter 5**
> "But you endure not patiently, nor fulfill the commandments of the Lord; but you transgress and calumniate his greatness; and malignant are the words in your polluted mouths against his Majesty. You withered in heart, no peace shall be to you!"
> 5. "Therefore your days shall you curse, and the years of your lives shall perish; perpetual execration shall be multiplied, and you shall not obtain mercy."[18]

If this is correct, that fallen angels observed and lusted after Adam and Eve, then *the eyes of both of them were opened, and they knew that they were naked* (Genesis 3:7 NASB) means that Adam and Eve for the first time understood both lust and how completely vulnerable they were to these creatures. The inadequate sewing together of fig leaves shows their feeble attempt to control lust. It also shows us how powerful this lust for the world system is.

IV. The Need For Atonement

A. God Is Not Responsible for Sin.

God not only agreed that Adam and Eve correctly understood the situation, but showed them that there was nothing they could do to atone for their sin. The LORD God killed an animal, an animal they might have been able to talk to, but which had to die to provide an adequate covering. This leather covering was necessary to atone for their sin as well as to hide their nakedness.

Also, *they knew that they were naked* the same way that later Adam *knew his wife Eve* and she bore children. The word "knew" is the same word in both instances and is the same in the *LXX* as well as the Hebrew. To *know* means both to understand and to experience. Adam understood lust, and in some way this understanding included experience.

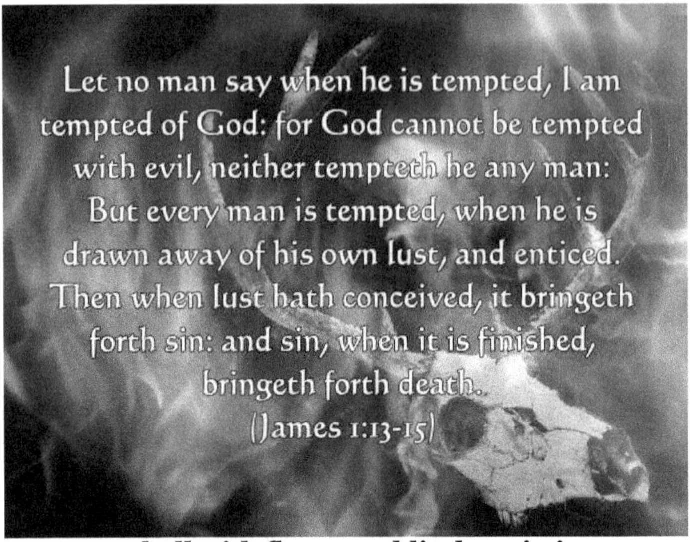

Deer skull with flames public domain image
“Let no man say when he is tempted, I am tempted of God: for God cannot be tempted with evil, neither tempteth he any man: But every man is tempted, when he is drawn away of his own lust, and enticed. Then when lust hath conceived, it bringeth forth sin: and sin, when it is finished, bringeth forth death.” (James 1:13-15)

The immediate result of Adam eating the fruit was the understanding of lust. The overwhelming desire to cover their nakedness might best be explained by the traditional belief that other spiritual beings walked in the garden. These other beings had already seen Adam and Eve naked, but Adam had just unleashed lust on the universe. Perhaps Adam was unaware of these previously invisible beings before he ate the fruit. He understood not only his own feelings and desires, but the changes in everyone and everything else.

It seems that the decision to rebel opened a pathway or at least a means of communication between our universe and this nonmaterial world of evil. Perhaps this gives us the real identity of the “ancient teachers of mankind” Graham Hancock speaks of. What he calls “ancient teachers” are not wise ancestors or even “good spirits” or “man’s collective memory”. Such “teachers” have their true identity in the being God warns us against in the Law of Moses, the source of the power promised through spiritism, witchcraft, and divination.

In the previous section the KJV very clearly and simply explains the LORD God’s prohibition against divination. This passage clearly shows that the antediluvian evil spirits exist after the flood. These material objects made into idols were not made because these were simple, ignorant people. These idols show that the power of evil spirits is very real and we need to understand that evil spirits can and do use material objects to influence our world for evil.

Public domain idol image

> *When thou art come into ha’aretz which Hashem Eloheicha giveth thee, thou shalt not learn to imitate the to’avot (abominations) of those Goyim. There shall not be found among you any one that maketh his ben or his bat to pass through the eish (i.e., be burned as an idol’s offering) or kosem kesamim (a diviner of divination) or a m’onen (soothsayer, astrologer), or a m’nachesh (one who interprets omens), or a mekhashshef (witch).*

> *Or one who casts spells, or one who inquires of a ghost or a familiar spirit, or a doresh el hamesim (a consulter of the dead ones, i.e., a necromancer). For all that do these things are a to'avat Hashem; and because of these to'evot, Hashem Eloheicha is about to drive them out before thee. Thou shalt be tamim (blameless) before Hashem Eloheicha.* (Deuteronomy 18: 9-13 Orthodox Jewish Bible)[19]

The common Secular Humanist (atheist) who reads this responds something like this: "Suppose I accept this story. Since you claim that God is all-knowing and all-powerful, he knew what would happen when he created Satan, Adam and Eve. Therefore God is responsible for creating evil. God cannot be a God of Love because He knew in advance that some people would reject Him and have to be sent to Hell. Therefore God is responsible for sending people to Hell."

> *I am the LORD, and there is none else, there is no God beside me: I girded thee, though thou hast not known me: That they may know from the rising of the sun, and from the west, that there is none beside me. I am the LORD, and there is none else. I form the light, and create darkness: I make peace, and create evil: I the LORD do all these things. Drop down, ye heavens, from above and let the skies pour down righteousness: let the earth open, and let them bring forth salvation, and let righteousness spring up together; I the LORD have created it. Woe unto him that striveth with his Maker!*

Morguefile image by Impure_with_memory of potter working small pot

> *Let the potsherd strive with the potsherds of the earth. Shall the clay say to him that fashioneth it, What makest thou? or thy work, He hath no hands? Woe unto him that saith unto his father, What begettest thou? or the woman, What hast thou brought forth?* (Isaiah 45:5-10, KJV)

Atheists are quick to point out that Isaiah wrote, *I make peace, and I create evil: I the LORD do all these things.* However, the same LORD that told Isaiah *I create evil* also told James *God cannot be tempted with evil, neither tempteth he any man.* God is sovereign, and as a sovereign LORD, He allows evil to exist and directs, or rather, overrules, the evil intents. *The LORD hath made all things for himself: yea, even the wicked for the day of evil* (Proverbs 16:4).

All the ancient records outside of the Bible that mention the Fall, such as the Jewish Babylonian Talmud and Josephus, add a great deal. It is easy to imagine the serpent saying something like, "See, everything is just like I told you. You haven't died and now you know good from evil." Here is a sample from the Jewish Encyclopedia.[20]

> Jewish theologians are divided in regard to the cause of this so-called "original sin"; some teach that it was due to Adam's yielding to temptation in eating of the forbidden fruit and has been inherited by his descendants; the majority, however, do not hold Adam responsible for the sins of mankind. The Zohar pictures Adam as receiving all the departed souls at his resting-place in the cave of Machpelah and inquiring of each soul the reason of its presence, whereupon the soul laments: "Woe unto me! thou art the cause of my departure from the world." Adam answers: "Verily, I have transgressed one precept and was punished; but see how many precepts and commandments of the Lord thou hast transgressed!" R. Jose said that every soul, before departing, visits Adam, and is convinced that it must blame its own wickedness, for there is no death without sin (*Zohar, Bereshit,* 57b).[20] (The *Zohar* is part of the *Kabbalah.*)
>
> The motive ascribed as underlying the prohibition against sin is the benefit of man. Sin defiles the body and corrupts the mind; it is a perversion and distortion of the principles of nature; it creates disorder and confusion in society; it brings mischief, misery, and trouble into communal life. Man, not God, reaps the benefit of obedience to God's laws: "If thou sinnest, what doest thou against him? . . . Thy wickedness may hurt a man as thou art" (Job xxxv. 6, 8).

The Bluecloud Dakota[21] have a Creation story that gives a humanist perspective quite opposed to the biblical account of Satan's rebellion and man's fall. It still has some interesting elements worth comparing. A brief summary of the various versions of the story follows.

Public Domain image woman with trickster mask

Early in the story two beings have a daughter who marries a god (Wind) and gives birth to the four winds. She and her parents become envious of the gods and want to become like them. The "Trickster" god makes their daughter proud of her beauty and she commits adultery with the Sun and causes a split between the Sun and the Moon, who were husband and wife.

Around this time men are created. The Trickster uses the daughter to lure some of them out of the cave where they were created with promises of clothing and food. They are deceived into believing beautiful, powerful, helpful beings live outside, and that food and clothing is easy to obtain. Those who leave are warned not to go and are told they can never return to the cave.[21]

Many Native American legends include a trickster. Few include any consciousness of sin or a "fall" story. The trickster might do things that are not good examples, but everyone enjoys laughing at his pranks and the humiliation he brings to others. Successfully tricking others is often considered a good character trait among many Native Americans. Sometimes human tricksters get advantages for themselves and their tribe. Stealing another tribe's horses, for example, is considered highly commendable.

B. God Is Good.

Though evil people and spirits are completely responsible for their own actions, the LORD will still overrule. This is brought out in the NASB: *I am the LORD, and there is no other, The One forming light and creating darkness, Causing well-being and creating CALAMITY; I am the LORD who does all these things* (Isaiah 45:6b-7). The LORD allows or permits evil, but overrules and channels calamities resulting from evil actions so that the result is that evil is judged. The clearest example of this in the Old Testament was God allowing the wicked Babylonians to execute His judgment on the wicked house of Judah.

So we know that *God is light* (good), a*nd in him is no darkness* (sin, evil) *at all.* (I John 1:5) At the end of the sixth day of Creation all creation, both the entire material universe and the entire spiritual creation were *very good.* (Genesis 1:31) Wickedness originated with Satan. Satan used the serpent to cause Eve to sin, who caused Adam to sin which caused sin to cross from the spiritual realm into the material realm which put the entire material universe under a curse.

C. God Provided Atonement

Hands on bouquet Photo by Alena Kratochvilova http://www.publicdomainpictures.net/

Marriage is perfect, complete type or illustration of our relationship with God. Marriage as defined by Adam and approved by Jesus the Messiah is not a fifty-fifty relationship. Each spouse is completely responsible and has 100% responsibility. It is a one hundred percent-one hundred percent relationship.

As each spouse in a marriage is completely responsible for the marriage, we are completely responsible for our relationship with God. Each and every person is 100% responsible for the decisions they make. At the same time God is 100% sovereign. Nothing is ever out of His control, even when the entire world went after witchcraft and diviners. The Spiritual aspect of this relationship is explained in the next two verses of Deuteronomy 18.

> *For these Goyim, which thou shalt dispossess, paid heed unto soothsayers, and unto diviners; but as for thee, Hashem Eloheicha hath not suffered thee so to do. Hashem Eloheicha will raise up unto thee a Navi [prophet] from among thee, of thy achim, kamoni (like me*

> *[Moshe, Ex 32:30]); unto him ye must listen;* (Deuteronomy 18:14,15, Orthodox Jewish Bible)[22]

> *For those nations, which you shall dispossess, listen to those who practice witchcraft and to diviners, but as for you, the Lord your God has not allowed you to do so. "The Lord your God will raise up for you a prophet like me from among you, from your countrymen, you shall listen to him."* (Deuteronomy 18:14,15, NASB)

When divination and witchcraft overwhelmed the world, God sent Moses with the promise of the Messiah.

> *And I will put eivah (enmity, Midrash Rabbah 23:5) between thee and HaIsha (see HaAlmah, Yeshayah 7:14), and between thy zera and her Zera; it shall crush thy rosh, and thou shalt strike his akev (heel).* (Genesis 3:15 Orthodox Jewish Bible)[23]

> *And I will put enmity between thee and the woman, and between thy seed and her seed; it shall bruise thy head, and thou shalt bruise his heel.* (Genesis 3:15 KJV)

Enmity means in this context continual, long-standing hatred. This is the warfare between good and evil which will be concluded with the Great White Throne Judgment when the heavens will be rolled up like a scroll (Isaiah 34:4) and God will create a new heaven and a new earth.

V. The Curse

A. The Serpent

> *The Lord God said to the serpent, "Because you have done this, Cursed are you more than all cattle, And more than every beast of the field; On your belly you will go, And dust you will eat All the days of your life; And I will put enmity Between you and the woman, And between your seed and her seed; He shall bruise you on the head, And you shall bruise him on the heel."* (Genesis 3:13,15 NASB)

This is both a genetic change in a material organism into a snake and an eternal conflict in the spiritual world between the seed of the woman and seed of the serpent. Though we cannot be certain, it is most likely two separate creatures or beings. These two creatures which exalted themselves were brought down in humiliation. The snake as a creature was cursed immediately and the seed of the serpent will be cursed at the final judgment.

The fight is to the death. But the best the seed of the serpent can do is to bruise, strike the heel of the seed of the woman. Satan did that with the crucifixion of the

Messiah. The Messiah, the seed of the woman, will eternally crush the head of the seed of Satan.

As the Messiah was a human born of a woman, so the seed of the serpent will somehow be material, almost certainly born of a woman. This seed of the serpent has yet to be revealed.

B. Eve

To the woman He said, "I will greatly multiply Your pain in childbirth, In pain you will bring forth children; Yet your desire will be for your husband, And he will rule over you." (Genesis 3:16 NASB)

Though the woman was named in the curse on the serpent, this aspect of the curse is specifically for Eve, the mother of all living, and her daughters. While some female mammals have painful births, it is uncommon. Most mammals give birth in thirty minutes to a few hours with few outward signs of pain. It seems to be a great deal of work for these other mammals, but nothing like the pain of a human childbirth.

Silhouette couple on beach photo by Andrew Schmidt http://www.publicdomainpictures.net/

Among liberals the desire of woman for her husband and family as well is entirely dismissed as nurture, a cultural norm, something which is taught or caught. Denial of this basic biological desire has resulted in massive alcohol abuse and drug abuse, both prescription and illegal drugs. Women are seventy percent more likely to have severe clinical depression than men. The seventy percent figure is based entirely on those women who seek professional medical treatment. There are estimates that women are ninety percent more depressed than men in Western cultures. The fashion and cosmetic industries are entirely built around female customers attempting to satisfy what they think are their personal needs.

This desire for a husband is not an evolutionary maternal instinct which some form of treatment can eliminate or reduce. But it is nothing compared to *he will rule over you*. Evil men have used this as an opportunity to exploit women in many ways. This power play or war of the sexes if you will, is the driving force in much, perhaps most, fiction. It is not simply physical or even psychological. It is hated and denied by liberals, especially feminists.

It is also a fact of life for women in cultures throughout history.

C. Everything Material

Then to Adam He said, "Because you have listened to the voice of your wife, and have eaten from the tree about which I commanded you, saying, 'You shall not eat from it'; Cursed is the ground because of you; In toil you will eat of it All the days of your life. "Both thorns and thistles it shall grow for you; And you will eat the plants of the field; By the sweat of your face You will eat bread, Till you return to the ground, Because from it you were taken; For you are dust, And to dust you shall return." (Genesis 3:17-19 NASB)

1. Adam Was Responsible

The LORD God was not only speaking to the man Adam. This curse is on the entire material existence of all living creatures. And more importantly, as head of a family, whatever happens to the husband also happens to the rest of the family. This is a curse on everyone in the entire human race, domesticated animals and eventually everything on earth. The only escape from this curse is to force someone else to do your work for you, either through slavery or purchasing their services.

Public domain image Fragment of the Book of Jubilees

The *Book of Jubilees*[24] is an ancient book which describes in more detail some of the events before the flood. Some Christians, such as the Coptic Church, believe the *Book of Jubilees* to be inspired Scripture. It accurately records the oldest Jewish traditions. However, we believe that it is not inspired and contains errors.

> And on that day on which Adam went forth from the Garden, he offered as a sweet savour an offering, frankincense, galbanum, and stacte, and spices in the morning with the rising of the sun from the day when he covered his shame. And on that day was closed the mouth of all beasts, and of cattle, and of birds, and of whatever walks, and of whatever moves, so that

> they could no longer speak: for they had all spoken one with another with one lip and with one tongue. And He sent out of the Garden of Eden all flesh that was in the Garden of Eden, and all flesh was scattered according to its kinds, and according to its types unto the places which had been created for them. And to Adam alone did He give (the wherewithal) to cover his shame, of all the beasts and cattle. On this account, it is prescribed on the heavenly tablets as touching all those who know the judgment of the law, that they should cover their shame, and should not uncover that is on the earth ... And as for all those who corrupted their ways and their thoughts before the flood.[24]

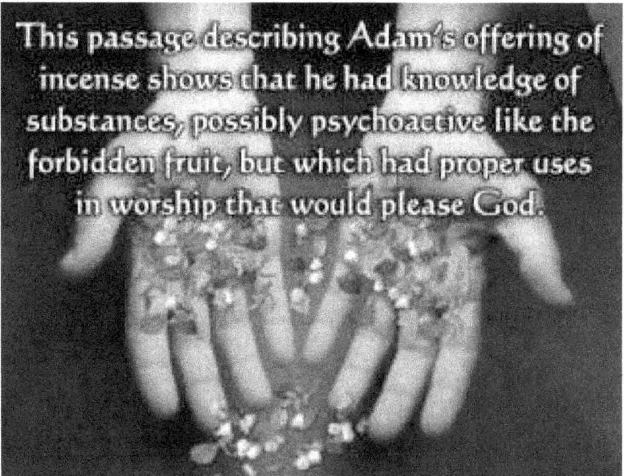

Hands dropping dried herbs, leaves public domain image

Compare this to the later discussion about knowledge imparted by the "sons of God" to their wives "the daughters of men" concerning such substances, and the discussion (p. 213) of the Aztec god Xochipilli ("Flower Prince").

The curse sets the guidelines or parameters for all of human history. Not only the human race, but also all of the material universe, is under the curse. *For we know that the whole creation groaneth and travaileth in pain together until now.* (Romans 8:22) The Bible only records the names of the first three sons of the first husband and wife, Adam and Eve. Cain (the firstborn) murdered Abel (the second born) in a fit of rage. Seth was born next, when Adam was 130 years old. The Bible then records that Adam and Eve had more sons and daughters. Jewish tradition tells us that Eve bore thirty-three sons and twenty-three daughters.[25]

2. Adam chose his wife over obedience to God.

Sometimes doing what is right is very difficult. Each and every one of us is faced with choices, many times each day. God could have made another woman to replace Eve. God could have even atoned for Eve's sin, though we do not know how. As difficult as that choice was for Adam, it was still a choice. And all choices have consequences.

3. The ground was cursed.

There is a common belief among Christians, Jews and even some Muslims that before the curse, all creatures only ate plants. Before Adam ate the forbidden fruit only plant cells died. Death of creatures with souls was introduced into the world by Adam's disobedience. Many also believe that before the Fall, eating was not necessary for survival; that it was strictly for fellowship and pleasure.

No longer would sufficient quantities of food grow on its own. Because of the curse men would need to cultivate the soil to produce food. Cultivation is a difficult process. It is painful as well as difficult and laborious.

4. Physical death

Till you return to the ground, Because from it you were taken; For you are dust, And to dust you shall return." Genesis 3:19 NASB

Ground and dust are general words. It means that we, each and every person, will have our bodies return to the individual chemicals which compose our bodies.

VI. Cain and Abel

A. The Purpose of Their Sacrifices

Since animals were not yet eaten as food (God permitted this after the flood), this first sacrifice was only for fellowship with the Lord God. As Keil and Delitzsch said, "We must bear in mind that the first sacrifices were offered after the fall, and therefore presupposed the spiritual separation of man from God, and were designed to satisfy the need of the heart for fellowship with God."[26]

Abel offered *"the firstlings of his flock and of their fat portions."* In other words, he offered the best of the best. Cain, however, offered *"the fruit of the ground."* The text shows a difference in attitude. Abel offered his best. Cain simply offered what he had. God was pleased with Abel's offering but *"had no regard"* for Cain's offering. God told Cain to do well and not allow sin to master him. Instead, he met Abel in a field and killed him.

Public domain image of Franz Delitzsch

B. Judgment of Cain

When God came to Cain, He first gave him the opportunity to repent by asking him where his brother Abel was. Cain denied his responsibility by asking, *"Am I my brother's keeper?"* He meant, "I'm not responsible for him."

There was no trial because God already knew the truth. He pronounced immediate judgment. The ground *"will no longer yield its strength to you; you will be a vagrant and a wanderer on the earth."* Cain understood this to be a death sentence, that not only would growing food be impossible, the animals, or perhaps his own brothers, would kill him. The important part of Cain's remorse was his comment *"and from thy face shall I be hid."* Though we have no information as to what the mark God gave Cain was, it somehow allowed Cain to live out a natural life.

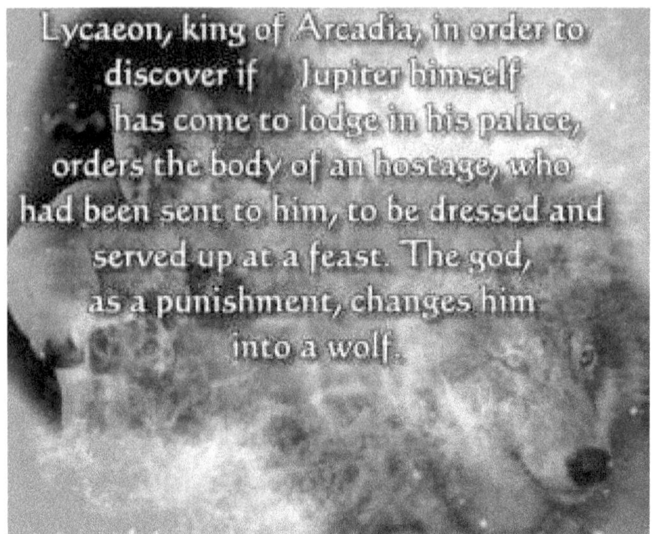

Public domain images man, wolf, swirling colored gasses Lycaeon, king of Arcadia, in order to discover if Jupiter himself has come to lodge in his palace, orders the body of a hostage, who had been sent to him, to be dressed and served up as a feast. The god, as punishment, changes him into a wolf.

Ovid's *Metamorphoses*[27] has a section about Lycaeon, king of Arcadia, who is supposed to have lived before the flood. One translator's note makes the observation in the illustration above. Lycaon was known for defying the gods, for being bloodthirsty and violent, and for being the first murderer. Whether he actually practiced cannibalism is uncertain but he was brazen enough to murder a man and serve him up as if he were to be eaten. The translator, admitting he cannot make a complete parallel, still finds some similarities to the story of Cain in this tale. He further comments that

> "It is just possible that the guilty Cain may have been the original of Lycaon. ... they are each mentioned as the first murderer; and the fact, that Cain murdered Abel at the moment when

> he was offering sacrifice to the Almighty, **[Author's note: The Scriptures do not actually seem to say that the murder happened at the same time of the sacrifice. This is an interpretation of the commentator.]** may have given rise to the tradition that Lycaon had set human flesh before the king of heaven. The Scripture, too, tells us, that Cain was personally called to account by the Almighty for his deed of blood.
>
> The punishment here inflicted on Lycaon was not very dissimilar to that with which Cain was visited. Cain was sentenced to be a fugitive and a wanderer on the face of the earth; and such is essentially the character of the wolf, shunned by both men and animals."[27]

This account of Lycaon both shows that some truth of the Word of God is contained in other ancient writings and how far these writing depart from the Word of God.

Cain was spared by God's mercy, and was able to *know* (have sexual relations with) his wife (A sister or niece. Such relations were not forbidden until the Mosaic Law), have children, move away from the presence of the Lord, east of Eden, to Nod, and to build a city. Ussher points out part of what Cain had to fear as consequences of murdering his brother.

> When Cain, the firstborn of all mankind, murdered Abel, God gave Eve another son called Seth. (Genesis 4:25) Adam had now lived 130 years. (Genesis 5:3) From whence it is gathered, that between the death of Abel and the birth of Seth, there was no other son born to Eve. For then, he should have been recorded to have been given her instead of him (This other son would have been mentioned instead of Seth). Since man had been on the earth 128

> years and Adam and Eve had other sons and daughters (Genesis 5:4) the number of people on the earth at the time of this murder could have been as many as 500,000. Cain might justly fear, through the conscience of his crime, that every man that met him would also slay him. (Genesis 4:14,15)

While some believe that building a city was rebellion against the Lord's judgment (that Cain would be a vagrant), it seems more likely that it was a natural result of needing to work harder to till the ground. It says the ground *"no longer yielded its strength,"* meaning cultivation and farming would require much more work. Cain would have to expend the additional effort required to build equipment, storage areas for the equipment, and storehouses to keep whatever he could manage to grow.

In some way before the additional curse on Cain, raising food was much easier. Perhaps the land closer to Eden was more fertile. It is also likely that Cain needed protection from the animals. His life was growing increasingly more difficult; with more physical labor and more dangers. It may be, according to Keil and Delitzsch, that the word translated *Enoch*, the name of Cain's firstborn as well as the name of his city, means *consecration* and is an act of repentance.[28] He still had to live with the consequences of his actions.

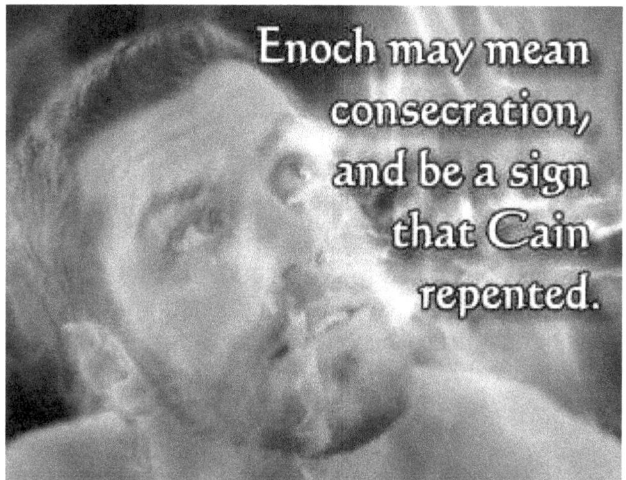

Public domain man in flames "Enoch may mean consecration, and be a sign that Cain repented."

The descendants of Cain began what we call civilization. Cain built the city of Enoch, named for his son. "City" does not mean skyscrapers and subways. It does mean people living close together with specialization of labor. That would require sewer systems, garbage disposal, a common water supply, streets, buildings, and some way of enforcing responsibility.

New Zealand has a legend which may echo Cain's record. Or this might be based on Lamech. Ruatapu became angry when his father Uenuku elevated his younger half-brother Kahutia-te-rangi ahead of him. Ruatapu lured Kahutia-te-rangi and a large number of young men of high birth into his canoe, and took them out to sea where he drowned them. He called on the gods to destroy his enemies and threatened to return as the great waves of early summer.[29]

> *And Lamech said unto his wives, Adah and Zillah, Hear my voice; ye wives of Lamech, hearken unto my speech: for I have slain a man to my wounding, and a young man to my*

> *hurt. If Cain shall be avenged sevenfold, truly Lamech seventy and sevenfold.* (Genesis 4:23)

Lamech's "sword song" shows the anger of his great-great-great grandfather Cain when he killed his brother Abel, but no evidence of repentance. For the first time in recorded human history, a man claims for himself the power of a god. Whatever the reason, Lamech brags to his wives (he is also the first polygamist) that he has murdered "a young man." He then boasts that he himself would take ten times the vengeance out on anyone who attempted to kill him for murdering the young man.

The date of Lamech's birth is not recorded. Since there were only 1656 years from the creation of Adam to beginning of the flood, and most men lived more than nine hundred years, Lamech probably died in the flood. The Lord told Noah, "*The end of all flesh is come before me; for the earth is filled with violence through them; and, behold, I will destroy them with the earth.*" Genesis 6:13. Unrepentant violence began with Lamech.

VII. Antediluvian Civilization

According to Josephus, Cain's great-great-grandson Lamech had seventy-seven children by two wives. These children of Lamech were inventors.

> *And Lamech took unto him two wives: the name of the one was Adah, and the name of the other Zillah. And Adah bare Jabal: he was the father of such as dwell in tents, and of such as have cattle. And his brother's name was Jubal: he was the father of all such as handle the harp and organ. And Zillah, she also bare Tubalcain, an instructor of every artificer in brass and iron.* (Genesis 4:19-22)

This implies that the other descendants of Adam slept either in the open, or in caves, since it is not recorded that they used either cities (buildings) or tents. For that to be possible, even the highest elevation on earth in the antediluvian world had to have a continuously mild climate. It also implies that shelter in lower elevations, either in a city or a tent, was necessary or desirable. Cain and his descendants lived east of Eden. Since water originated in Eden and flowed downhill, Cain and his descendants lived at a lower elevation.

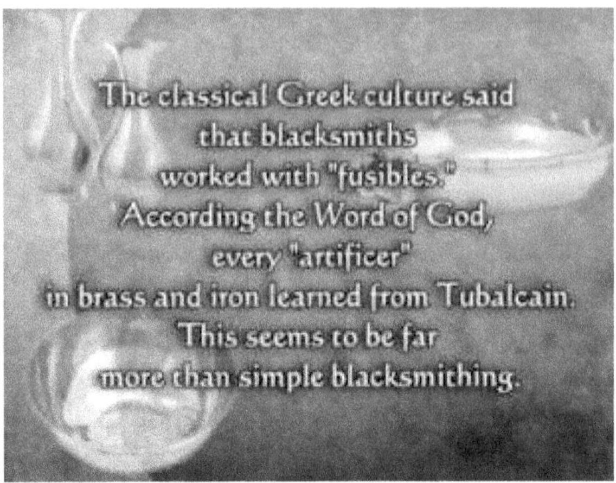

Public domain images of golden vessels on stucco background. The classical Greek culture said that blacksmiths worked with "fusibles." According to the Word of God, every "artificer" in brass and iron learned from Tubalcain. This seems to be far more than simple blacksmithing.

Lamech's son Jabal was the father of such as dwell in tents and such as have cattle. Since tents were made out of leather and God had not yet given permission to eat meat, Jabal founded the leather industry. His brother Jubal discovered or invented the harp (stringed instruments) and pipes, that is, instruments which have a column of vibrating air. The KJV word *organ* can include all of what we think of as brass and woodwind instruments. It can include bagpipes, recorders, trumpets, bugles, oboes, clarinets and anything else with a column of air. The word harp is more limited. It only means what we think of as a harp or a lyre.

Public domain image of Sumerian Kings List

The Ancient Sumerians also made a list of men who supposedly reigned before the flood. It is not considered important because most translations have 8 kings reigning 241,200 years. However, Raúl Erlando López believes that the Sumerian King List is not translated correctly.

> "The lives of the biblical patriarchs, however, have a precision of one year. If Adam and Noah are not included (as in the King List), and the lives of the patriarchs are similarly rounded to two digits, the sum of the lives has six 103 signs, six 102 signs and six 10 signs. In addition, if the number representing the sum of the ages was wrongly assumed as having been written in the sexagesimal system, the two totals become numerically equivalent.
>
> It is suggested that the Sumerian scribe that composed the original antediluvian list had available a document (possibly a clay tablet) containing numerical information on the ages of eight of the patriarchs similar to that of the Genesis record and that he mistakenly interpreted it as being written in the

sexagesimal system."[32]

J. Walton also made this assumption and came to the following conclusion.

> "If Adam and Noah are dropped from the biblical list, the number of people in the two lists is then the same: eight. Walton has also noticed that the total of the durations of the kingdoms and the total of the ages of the patriarchs are numerically related and are equivalent if the number base of the Sumerian list is changed from sexagesimal to decimal."
>
> This simply means that, if the assumption that the Sumerian King list is in decimal is correct, that it matches the Genesis 5 chronology between Adam and Noah."[32]

God Calls Enoch and Noah

VIII. God Calls Enoch and Noah

Public domain release by author Jack 1956 Wikimedia Commons. Cuneiform tablet with the Atra-Hasis Epic in the British Museum

The Mesopotamian *Epic of Atrahasis* speaks about the majority of the population refusing to worship the same god this counterpart of Noah serves. It echoes the biblical idea that only Noah was found faithful in all the earth.

> Atrahasis received the command.
> He assembled the Elders at his gate.
> Atrahasis made ready to speak,
> and said to the Elders:
> "My god does not agree with your god,
> Enki and Enlil are constantly angry with each other.
> They have expelled me from the land.
> Since I have always reverenced Enki,
> he told me this.
> I cannot live in ...
> Nor can I set my feet on the earth of Enlil.
> I will dwell with my god in the depths.
> This he told me: ..."[31]

Atrahasis appears to be a leader of men, calling together the important men of the city to deliver the message of coming destruction. Scholars interpret other fragmentary ancient works to mean that he became a ruler of men. Scholars speculate that he was, in the context of this myth, once man was created, the leader designated by the gods to take over as overseer of the tasks the lesser gods formerly did.

Noah is sometimes credited with being a ruler in his day. The New Testament certainly credits him with being a *"preacher of righteousness"* and therefore having some ability to get men of that day to listen to his words.

The genealogical record does not include Cain, but goes back to Adam through Seth. God says that in Seth's time *"men began to call upon the name of the Lord."* Seth's genealogical record includes Enoch, the man who, like Elijah, never died. *And Enoch walked with God: and he was not; for God took him*. (Genesis 5:24) His son Methuselah lived to be nine-hundred-sixty-nine years old and died just before the beginning of the flood.

Myths Deliberately Falsify History

IX. Myths Deliberately Falsify History

Public domain image of Dr. David Livingston, Jr.

Secular Humanists might object to not including more sources, especially in this section. Dr. David Livingston answers this complaint. The following explains why we do not "support" or "prop up" the accuracy of the Scriptures with other ancient works, but only cite them when they agree with and contain kernels of the same the truth already expressed in the Bible. (Dr. Livingston's Article is on p. 613.) [32]

> "The myths and epics of the ancient near east are fabricated religio-politico documents with a calculated purpose. They did not 'evolve' as

bards sang them around campfires ..."Being the "son of the god" (a different god in each city), he (the supreme ruler) owned everything, along with the priesthood. Thus he could take anything he wished from the people.

Ezra
and
Nehemiah
read aloud
and
explained
the Torah
to a huge crowd

Public domain scroll image "Ezra and Nehemiah read aloud and explained the Torah to a huge crowd."

Just as Ezra and Nehemiah read aloud and explained the Torah to a huge crowd (Neh 8:1 - 9:3), likewise the pagans did the same with their literature. Documents contrived by scribes and priests were intended to be read aloud to all the people at various festivals (op. cit.: 96, 100-01, 191-92). After the religious brainwashing, they may have given anything the king wished. When men have forsaken Absolute Truth (or never have known Him), all that is left is fantasy; a dream world. Rousas Rushdonny makes the point,

> The myth reveals a hatred of history . . . The purpose man then sets for himself in his myths is to end history, to make man the absolute governor by decreeing an end to the movement that is history. Where his myths acknowledge man's lot in history, man ascribes his sorry role, not to his depravity, but to the jealousy of the gods. The goal of the myth, progressively more clearly enunciated in time, has become the destruction of history and the enthronement of man as the new governor of the universe (1967: 1).

Thus, one should see the myths and epics for what they are: a deliberate attempt by ambitious and evil men (under the leadership of evil spiritual influences) to subjugate the populace and extort from them, along with the supporting priest-nobles, all that is needed for the most voluptuous lifestyle. When man becomes completely degenerate, he will develop a system to support his degeneracy. Occasionally a ruler might be more lenient with the people. But, none ever relinquishes divine kingship.[32]

The quote from Rousas Rushdonny bears repeating.

> "Where his myths acknowledge man's lot in history, man ascribes his sorry role, not to his depravity, but to the jealousy of the gods. The goal of the myth, progressively more clearly enunciated in time, has become the destruction of history and the enthronement of man as the new governor of the universe."

A god, Ifa, tired of living on earth
and went to dwell in the firmament.
Without his assistance,
mankind couldn't interpret the desires
of the gods, and one god [Olokun],
in a fit of rage, destroyed nearly
everybody in a great flood.

Public domain images ofstylized flood waters. "A god, Ifa, tired of living on earth and went to dwell in the firmament. Without his assistance, mankind coldn't interpret the desires of the gods, and one god, [Olokun], in a fit of rage, destroyed nearl everybody in a great flood."

The Yoruba people have a preflood legend 1(summarized in the graphic above) underscoring the character of many myths by stating that man cannot understand the will of the gods without a guide, someone who lives among them and claims divine origin. (The endnote also sources the quote in the graphic above.)[33]

New York Public Library "From the Earth and its inhabitants, Africa. Elisee Reclus (1830-1905) Public Domain Wikimedia Commons. Yoruba Trader

This should sound familiar. The people brought in by the Assyrians to repopulate the Northern Kingdom had the same attitude.

> *And the king of Assyria brought men from Babylon, and from Cuthah, and from Ava, and from Hamath, and from Sepharvaim, and placed them in the cities of Samaria instead of the children of Israel: and they possessed Samaria, and dwelt in the cities thereof. And so it was at the beginning of their dwelling there, that they feared not the LORD: therefore the LORD sent lions among them, which slew some*

of them. Wherefore they spake to the king of Assyria, saying, The nations which thou hast removed, and placed in the cities of Samaria, know not the manner of the God of the land: therefore he hath sent lions among them, and, behold, they slay them, because they know not the manner of the God of the land. Then the king of Assyria commanded, saying, Carry thither one of the priests whom ye brought from thence; and let them go and dwell there, and let him teach them the manner of the God of the land. Then one of the priests whom they had carried away from Samaria came and dwelt in Bethel, and taught them how they should fear the LORD. (II Kings 17:24-28)

X. False Religions Designed to Absolve Humans.

The history of man outside of the Scriptures, then, is self-justification. If he must include the truth about his fallen nature, he explains it away by saying, “It’s the gods’ fault, not mine.” In this way lust, greed, self-indulgence, and enslavement of the whole world, are justified as “divine rights.” Man becomes a god unto himself. He often sets his own standards for good works and then relies on them to justify himself.

A. Confucianism

Confucianism[34] is one of the best and easiest to understand examples of a man-made religion that exalts man’s earthly efforts and achievements, and the supposed “unknowable” nature of god and heaven. (The graphic below shows Confucius’ Rongo Dialects.)

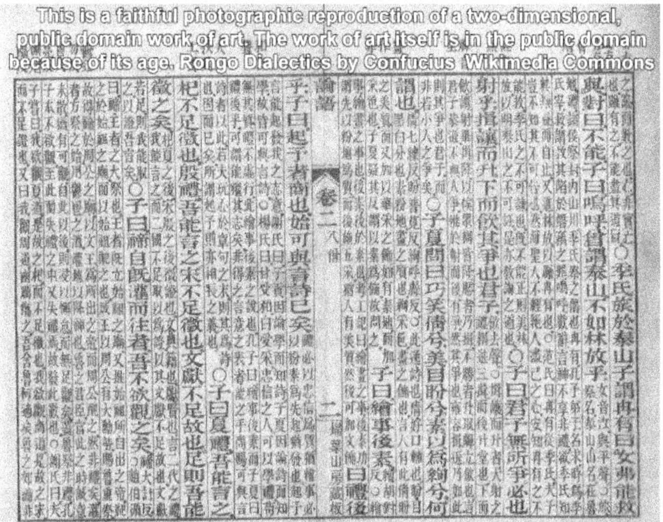

This is a faithful photographic reproduction of a two-dimensional public domain work of art. The work of art itself is in the public domain because of its age. Rongo Dialectics by Confucius. Wikimedia Commons.

> [It] concentrates on appropriate behavior in life, not a future heaven. The afterlife is unknowable, so all effort should be made to make this life the best it can be, to honor ancestors, and to respect elders.[34]

B. Hinduism

Hinduism[35] speaks of "The Four Goals of Life," dharma (righteousness), artha (worldly prosperity or material well-being), kama (enjoyment or pleasure), and moksha (liberation).

(The article referenced contains much more information on Hindu beliefs. It also has an interesting attempt to compare them to Christianity)

> Three ways have been prescribed by which one may attain perfection, or be liberated from the bondage of Samsara. They are as follows:
> The Karma Yoga, i.e., the path of work
> The Jnana Yoga, i.e., the path of knowledge
> The Bhakti Yoga, i.e., the path of devotion

Hindu writings are very difficult to understand but, in spite of the contention below that "Moksha" (the chief goal of life) cannot be "produced", clearly works are necessary to achieve these goals. Hinduism's life goals include seeking prosperity, exhaustive study of its billions of words of teaching texts, and performing good deeds.

> "Freedom from Samsara, the cycle of birth and death, is moksha. It implies union with Brahman: the only Absolute Reality. By this experience of Brahman, avidya (ignorance) is destroyed. By the power of Maya one is deceived into believing that the plurality of phenomenon is true. In his avidya he is chained to samara, the manifest world filled with the cycle of events, of birth, death, rebirth, etc. Moksha is the eternal, intrinsic nature of the Atman and is the chief goal of life. It can neither be produced, modified, attained, nor refined since it is an accomplished fact, the intrinsic nature of the Atman that needs to be discovered by intuition. Self-realization or realization of the Atman (Self) as the reality of the universe is moksha. The key is detachment from the phenomenal world and union with Absolute Reality."[35]

C. Buddhism

Buddhism[36] promises eventual Nirvana in ways similar to Hinduism, through good deeds and reincarnation. More information is available in the appendix.

> "a clear doctrine of salvation in the Buddha's teachings: Salvation in early Buddhism was nirvana, the extinguishing of the all karma that constitutes the self. Nirvana is not a place or a state, but the end of rebirth ... The Buddha said little about nirvana, because he felt that the alleviation of suffering was far more important, and that focusing on the goal of ultimate salvation would only lead to more attachments, and therefore more suffering. Rather than focus on nirvana as a goal, therefore, lay Buddhists were encouraged to give donations of goods, services, or money to monks or monasteries; to chant or copy sutras; and to engage in other activities in order to gain merit that could lead to a more desirable rebirth, which would bring them closer to enlightenment."[36]

Public domain image of Ho Tai "Happy Buddah"

The Roman Catholic Church

D. The Roman Catholic Church

The Roman Catholic Church teaches that baptism (among other deeds listed as *sacraments*) is necessary for salvation, making it one of many religions that teach works or human effort is necessary for salvation. This is from the *Catholic Catechism*. (The endnote also sources the text in the graphic below.)[37]

Catholic Catechism 1257
The Lord himself affirms that
Baptism is necessary for salvation.
He also commands his disciples to
proclaim the Gospel to all
nations and to baptize them. Baptism
is necessary for salvation for those to
whom the Gospel has been proclaimed
and who have had the possibility
of asking for this sacrament.
The Church does not
know of any means other than Baptism
that assures entry into eternal beatitude;
this is why she takes care not to neglect
the mission she has received from the Lord
to see that all who can be baptized are
"reborn of water and the Spirit." God has
bound salvation to the sacrament of
Baptism, but he himself is not bound
by his sacraments.

Catholic Catechism 1257

"The Lord Himself affirms that Baptism is necessary for salvation. He also commands His disciples to proclaim the Gospel to all nations and baptize them. Baptism is necessary for salvation for those to whom the Gospel has been proclaimed and who have had the possibility of asking for this sacrament. The Church does not know of any means other than Baptism that assures entry into eternal beatitude; this is why she takes care not to neglect the mission she has received from the Lord to see that all who can be baptized are "reborn of water and the Spirit." God has bound salvation to the sacrament of Baptism, but he himself is not bound by his sacraments."

E. The Quran

The Quran is the basis of the Islamic religion. Like all religions, Islam promises salvation through works. The appendix also includes more basic information on Islam.

> Paradise be brought near unto the Pious: "This is what ye have been promised: to every one who hath turned in penitence to God and kept his laws; Who hath feared the God of Mercy in secret, and come to him with a contrite heart: Enter it in peace: this is the day of Eternity."
>
> "This is Paradise, which ye have received as your heritage in recompense for your works."[38]

The politically-created false gods are capricious, not to be relied on, but worshiped out of fear. They admire demigods and heroic figures like Gilgamesh, Hercules, and Achilles, and get them to fight their battles and recover their lost possessions. They inflict punishments when outwitted or when their lustful desires are rebuffed. These repeated tales of gods seducing or trying to seduce mortals echo the lust of the sons of God in Genesis or the fallen angels of the *Book of Enoch*.

XI. God's Judgment on the Antediluvian World

A. Who Are the Sons of God?

According to Bible Commentators Keil and Delitzsch, three theories exist about the possible meaning of "the sons of God" and "the daughters of men" in Genesis 6:2.

Three different views have been entertained from the very earliest times: the "sons of God" being regarded as

(a) the sons of princes,

(b) angels,

(c) the Sethites or godly men; and

the "daughters of men," as the daughters

(a) of people of the lower orders,

(b) of mankind generally,

(c) of the Cainites, or of the rest of mankind as contrasted with the godly or the children of God.

Keil and Delitzsch themselves, interestingly enough, take different positions on this.

1. The Sons of Princes

They dismiss the idea that these were just princes or rulers. More of their lengthy commentary on this can be found in the appendix.[39] A number of authors of older writings took this view, but nothing contained any solid evidence or even solid reasoning to support this position.

2. Corruption of the Godly Line of Seth

Pastor Don Adams of Trinity Baptist Church, Weatherly PA, a friend of the authors' who holds to the Sethite position, provided an articulate explanation of this belief.

> I agree with Evans that the sons of God (Hebrew =ben elohim) in Genesis 6:2, 4 are the sons of Seth. This seems to be the best interpretation in the context (Gen 5 speaks of Seth's offspring, not fallen angels). As men got further from God the Sons of Seth (Godly line), (Note: How Eve refers to Seth (Gen 4:25-26)) started to take daughters of men (Cainites). The fallen angels view I believe runs into the problem of where their offspring got their sin nature. Man's Sin nature was passed down from Adam not fallen angels. It is possible they may have been demon-possessed. But the seed still came from these fallen men.
>
> In Job 1:6; 2:1; 34:7 the sons of God (Hebrew=ben elohim) seem to be angels among whom Satan comes in Job 1:6; 2:1 to present himself before God. So my take is the context must be taken into account wherever the phrase "Sons of God" is used. In the New Testament the phrase "Sons of God" always refers to believers.

Authors' personal photo of Trinity Baptist Church.

I do believe at least some fallen angels (there are different orders of both holy angels and fallen) are demons. Interesting question, whether angels have a sin nature. I cannot think of any Scripture that teaches it like it does clearly for men. They certainly are sinful in that they rebelled with Satan and left their first estate and are destined for the Lake of Fire. But Scripture does not call them sinners specifically like it does man. So I don't see how we can equate fallen angels having a sinful nature like man. They all are confirmed in their personal choice. It is for Adam's race who passed on his sin nature that Jesus died to forgive and transform. It is to mankind the Gospel is preached not fallen angels. Paul is probably the source of Evans and others who say the Gentiles worship demons as their gods (1 Co 10:20). The problem I have with FALLEN angels cohabiting with women and having children is that the Bible clearly states our sin nature is passed down through Adam and his seminal descendants. Mankind from Adam on are held accountable for their sin nature and sin (Rom 5:12ff) not fallen angels. I know what others teach on this. But I do not see any justification in Scripture for the fallen angel view. I cannot reconcile it with the Scripture's teaching on man's sinfulness or the doctrine of the Virgin Birth of Jesus Christ which rests on the fact that Jesus had no sinful nature because the seed of His conception was from the Holy Spirit not man. Satan I believe fell after the Creation which I believe included the Garden of Eden. Sometime after Creation Satan fell and then tempted Eve in the Garden. It seems to me

> Adam and Eve were in the Garden of Eden some time before they fell.[40]

This also seems to be the position of many Messianic Jews and many of the Reformers. From the Reformation period until the early twentieth century, this was the near-universal position of the Church.

3. Fallen Angels

Whiston's translation of Josephus' *Antiquities* includes a note (see the second paragraph preceded by 11 below) that follows the quoted text.

> For many angels (11) of God accompanied with women, and begat sons that proved unjust, and despisers of all that was good, on account of the confidence they had in their own strength; for the tradition is, that these men did what resembled the acts of those whom the Grecians call giants.
>
> (11) This notion, that the fallen angels were, in some sense, the fathers of the old giants, was the constant opinion of antiquity.[41]

William Whiston's phrase "the constant opinion of antiquity" means the universal opinion of antiquity. While universal does not mean unanimous, it was the overwhelming majority opinion. The twentieth century saw Christians returning the ancient belief that the sons of God were fallen angels.

The *Book of Enoch* tells of 200 angels/sons of heaven who "vowed together to get human wives and children by them and hoped by banding together to escape punishment."[42] This is a thread running through much of ancient literature. Even the fallen angels apparently knew something about the Atonement: the future coming of the One Who would redeem mankind. Some commentators interpret Eve's statement at the birth of Cain, "I have gotten a

man from the Lord." as meaning she believed she had given birth to *the Man*, the Messiah.

B. Similarities to the Biblical Record in Other Sources

The history of mankind as written down in ancient documents contains partial truths of God's original revelation, including the promised redeemer. So the counterfeits invented by "divine rulers" would ring true in the minds of those distant from the source of truth. This is how the false divine ruler comes into a society. He claims to be the son of a god, to speak for the god, to be "sent by his father" to tell us what the god wants us to do, not to truly be redeemed, but to sweep sin under the rug.

Fallen man has long believed in a corrupted version of Genesis 3:15. Most, if not every, culture has "the Chosen One," a being born by a union of the spiritual and physical. Of course they have no desire to submit to the true God and His Son. They instead create so-called "prophecies" based on a grain of truth about Jesus Christ.

1. Assyrian[43]

The Assyrian record of the god Zu includes a passage that may echo this story of angels lusting after and seducing women, corrupting them with cosmetics and material wealth.

> 10. his wife forcibly he associated with,
> 12. in companionship he made sit.
> 16. the goddess of perfumes a female fashioned? of her mother in her likeness
> 17. Her appearance was like bright ukni stone,
> 18. her girdle was adorned with silver and gold...[43]

2. Zoroastrian (ancient Persian)

Zoroastrianism[44] records a story about the first king, or Shah. This may speak of Satan's rebellion against God or his jealousy of man and attacks against him. It describes how early man grew in knowledge, technology, and prosperity, but also records the attacks of the evil enemy seeking to overthrow him. The epic records how magical beings and even beasts were used in this battle, hinting at the spiritual and physical aspects of man's early history on Earth.

Images of The Epic of Kings by Ferdowski illustration from Bullfinch's Mythology; Persian Daric coin Spurlock Museum University of Illinois at Urbana Champaign Public Domain

> Kaiumers first sat upon the throne of Persia, and was master of the world. He took up his abode in the mountains, ... from him sprang all kindly nurture and the arts of clothing, till then unknown. Men and beasts from all parts of the earth came to do him homage and receive laws at his hands, and his glory was like to the sun. Then Ahriman the Evil, when he saw how the

> Shah's honour was increased, waxed envious, and sought to usurp the diadem of the world.[44]

3. *Book of Jubilees*

The *Book of Jubilees*[45] records its version of the sins of man that led up to the flood.

> He was moreover with the angels of God ... and they showed him everything which is on earth and in the heavens, ... He testified to the Watchers, who had sinned with the daughters of men; for these had begun to unite themselves, so as to be defiled, with the daughters of men, and Enoch testified against (them) all. And he was taken from amongst the children of men, and we conducted him into the Garden of Eden in majesty and honour, and behold there he writes down the condemnation and judgment of the world, and all the wickedness of the children of men. And on account of it (God) brought the waters of the flood upon all the land.[45]

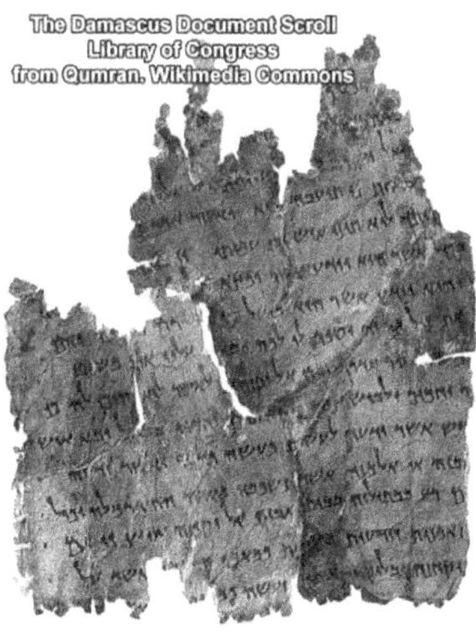

The Damascus Document scroll Library of Congress from Qumran, Wikimedia Commons

4. The Zadokite or Damascus Document

The Zadokite or Damascus Document[46] is not Scriptures but it speaks about conditions before the flood in a way that agrees with Scriptures.

> And now, children, listen to me, and I will open your eyes to see and understand how God acts, so that you may choose what He has desired and reject what He has hated, walking blamelessly in all His ways and not straying after thoughts of guilty lust or after whoring eyes. For many there be that have strayed thereby from olden times until now, and even strong heroes have stumbled thereby. (Endnote also references text in graphic.)

Image of Watcher created using Poser 3D elements

> So too their sons, whose height was like the lofty cedars and whose bodies were as mountains. They also fell.

> So too 'all flesh that was upon the dry land'. They also perished These became as though they had never been, because they did their own pleasure and kept not the commandments of their Maker. In the end His anger was kindled against them.[46]

5. Mesoamerican

Cultures around the world worshiped gods who had sexual relationships with humans. These gods are often married, yet they introduce sexual sins. Xochipilli was the Aztec god of art, games, beauty, dance, flowers, and song. His wife was believed to be a human girl named Mayahuel. He was one of the gods responsible for fertility and agricultural produce. The Toltec civilization seems to have revered Xochipilli as a god favoring homosexuals and male prostitutes. Note the discussion later about his association with psychotropic substances. Expanded resource for Xochipilli click here).[47]

6. Gurarani

Kurupi is a god in Guarani mythology blamed for unexpected or unwanted pregnancies. (The Guaraní people live in south-central part of South America, especially in Paraguay and parts of the surrounding areas of Argentina, Brazil, and Bolivia.) The Pombero is a creature similar to descriptions of this god. Both were used to excuse adultery or explain ugly, excessively hairy, or otherwise deformed children. They were also blamed for the disappearance of young women. Instead of taking responsibility for immorality, adultery, rape, or kidnapping, these people invented a "divine" being to excuse their sin. This invention might have even been used to justify abortion or exposure of unwanted or imperfect children.[48]

7. Hindu

The Hindu god Kamadeva/Madana[49] has a consort Rati, "whose very essence is desire." Sometimes he has two wives, Rati and Priti. He is spoken of as sneaking into Shiva's meditation chamber and, Cupid-like, shooting Shiva with an arrow intended to make him awaken and desire his wife. Shiva destroyed him for this invasion but resurrected him as a spirit being capable of spreading sexual desire throughout the world. He successfully tempted Shiva to give up meditation and unite with his wife to produce a child that would save the gods from an attack.[49]

Hindu god depiction from Image from World Photo Cube

8. Norse

Freyr, a Norse god, was associated with "sacral kingship" (being a priest, judge, and a ruler), virility and prosperity, with sunshine and fair weather, and was pictured as a fertility god. Freyr "bestows peace and pleasure on mortals". He is sometimes said to be an ancestor of the Swedish royal house.[50]

9. Plato

In Plato's Socratic dialogue *Cratylus,*[51] they discuss the origin of demons.

> Socrates: Demons! And what do you consider to be the meaning of this word? ... Hesiod ... speaks of a golden race of men who came first?

> ... But now that fate has closed over this race
> They are holy demons upon the earth,
> Beneficent, averters of ills, guardians of mortal men. ... Why, I suppose that he means by the golden men, not men literally made of gold, but good and noble; and I am convinced of this, because he further says that we are the iron race. ... I have the most entire conviction that he called them demons, because they were daemones (knowing or wise), and in our older Attic dialect the word itself occurs. Now he and other poets say truly, that when a good man dies he has honour and a mighty portion among the dead, and becomes a demon; which is a name given to him signifying wisdom. And I say too, that every wise man who happens to be a good man is more than human (daimonion) both in life and death, and is rightly called a demon.[51]

Public Domain greek statue

Socrates claims by this argument that demons are good and wise "golden" helpers of men. It would be easy to say he is only speaking of men, but he makes it clear he refers to the power these men have “in life and death”, implying that they are other than mortal beings. He also has an answer for the question of where heroes (the biblical “mighty men of old, men of renown”) came from.

> All of them sprang either from the love of a God for a mortal woman, or of a mortal man for a Goddess; think of the word in the old Attic, and you will see better that the name heroes is only a slight alteration of Eros, from whom the heroes sprang.[51]

10. Ovid[52]

“Thus when the God, **whatever God was he,** Had form’d the whole ... “ says Ovid in the *Metamorphoses,* echoing the idea of this unknown and unknowable god. From the very first days of creation the “lesser” gods seem to be out of control, destructive, selfish.

Statue of Ovid by Ettore Ferrari (1845-1929) Photo by Romeo Tabus Wikimedia Commons

> Thunder's voice, which wretched mortals fear, and winds that on their wings cold winter bear. Nor were those blust'ring brethren left at large, On seas, and shores, their fury to discharge: Bound as they are, and circumscrib'd in place, They rend the world, resistless, where they pass; And mighty marks of mischief leave behind; Such is the rage of their tempestuous kind ... wanton Zephyr wings his flight; Pleas'd with the remnants of departing light: Fierce Boreas, with his off-spring, issues forth T' invade the frozen waggon of the North. While frowning Auster seeks the Southern sphere; And rots, with endless rain, th' unwholesome year.[52]

But Ovid reassures the reader that a "better" creation is coming, and that man's essence includes divine energy. The true God gave the breath of life to man. He formed man in His own image. This truth is perverted all around the world in myths that claim the divine creative energy actually makes man have the nature of a god.

> A creature of a more exalted kind Was wanting yet, and then was Man design'd: Conscious of thought, of more capacious breast, For empire form'd, and fit to rule the rest: Whether with particles of heav'nly fire The God of Nature did his soul inspire, Or Earth, but new divided from the sky, And, pliant, still retain'd th' aetherial energy: Which wise Prometheus temper'd into paste, And, mixt with living streams, the godlike image cast. Thus, while the mute creation downward bend Their sight, and to their earthly mother tend, Man looks aloft; and with erected eyes Beholds his own hereditary skies. From such rude principles our form began; And earth was metamorphos'd into Man.[120]

Ovid includes tales of sexual seduction right after the flood and involves Jove himself, implying that this wickedness was nothing new and was the norm before the flood as well. In the Greco-Roman flood legends, Jove (Greek Zeus) felt justified in destroying the world because the text doesn't mention sexual license as being immorality. Sexual obsession is a very early form of immortality: in *The Book of Enoch* it dates from the time of Enoch's father Jared, when these angels made this vow. In a biblical context and in Greek myths this is before the flood.

11. *Book of Enoch*

According to the *Book of Enoch*, The angels introduced their human wives to psychotropic drugs. "They taught them charms and enchantments, and the cutting of roots, and made them acquainted with plants."[53] Humans were encouraged to transcend the natural world, to "ascend." It became part of man's quest to "evolve". Man's sinful nature has always included the desire to go beyond traditional moral constraints. Free love, open marriage, and other kinds of sexual exploration are all considered by secularists today to be "necessary" for man's evolution. Man had these ideas since ancient times, and used to call it "communion with the gods".

Men brought the flood upon themselves as a result of lust: all kinds of materialism. Extreme and wrong desires or lusts resulted in warfare, misuse of metallurgy and weapons technology, excessive ornamentation and makeup. Antimony[54] is a silvery or black metallic element used in cosmetics, extremely common in the ancient world. (Kohl). It can have poisonous properties similar to arsenic, causing liver damage, and also may have emetic properties. Excessive exposure can cause loss of mental clarity as well as serious health problems. It may have been one of the ancient drugs used by Satan or his human agents to control the populace and to create dependency.

Photo by Keith Schengili-Roberts
Kohl cosmetic tube inscribed with the
cartouches of Amenhotep III and Queen Tiye.
1 February 2007 Brooklyn Museum
Wikimedia Commons

Photo by Keith Schengili-Roberts Kohl cosmetic tube inscribed with the cartouches of Amenhotep III and Queen Tiye. 1 Feb. 200 Brooklyn Museum Wikimedia Commons

12. Entheogen

Entheogen[55] means "the god within" and refers to the use of psychotropic drugs to create spiritual experiences. They have been used for millennia in religious rituals, spiritually-based attempts at healing, "out of body" experiences, and by those who claim to reveal the will of the gods. Peyote, psilocybin mushrooms, uncured tobacco, cannabis, and many other plant products have been used to produce these effects.

13. Aztec

A 16th-century Aztec statue[56] of the god Xochipilli ("Prince of Flowers") was found near Tlalmanalco. Both the statue and the base are covered with carvings of psychoactive plants, including mushrooms, tobacco, and others. The figure has its head tilted upward. Its eyes are hollow-looking, the mouth half open, hands raised. It seems to be in a drug-induced state.

Xochipilli public domain image. The statue is in the Museo Nacional de Antropología in Mexico City

C. Judgment on Wicked Spirits

Very little is written in the Word of God about the judgment on evil spirits, except that it happened.

> *And the angels which kept not their first estate, but left their own habitation, he hath reserved in everlasting chains under darkness unto the judgment of the great day.* Jude 6

> *For Christ also hath once suffered for sins, the just for the unjust, that he might bring us to God, being put to death in the flesh, but quickened by the Spirit: By which also he went and preached unto the spirits in prison; Which sometime were disobedient, when once the longsuffering of God waited in the days of Noah, while the ark was a preparing, wherein*

> *few, that is, eight souls were saved by water.* (1 Peter 3:18-20)

Man had metalworking and other technologies by the time of Lamech (Cain's immediate descendants). He didn't need to get that knowledge from the angels. However, he still sought and was given occult knowledge which led him into sin. It also meant death for men to learn and use these arts.

1. *Book of Enoch*

They would eventually share the punishment of the rebellious angels, perhaps described in the *Book of Enoch* below.

> "And again the Lord said to Raphael: "Bind Azâzêl hand and foot, and cast him into the darkness: and make an opening in the desert, which is in Dûdâêl, and cast him therein. And place upon him rough and jagged rocks, and cover him with darkness, and let him abide there forever, and cover his face that he may not see light."[57]

This passage parallels the casting out of Satan. The place where Azâzêl is confined is said in the *Book of Enoch* to be under modern Babylon, Iran and Iraq.

The condemned watchers of the *Book of Enoch* ask him to intercede for them and he has a vision of taking their petition to God. God says they should intercede for men, not men for them. This is evidence of their continuing self-centeredness. (The image has another quote from Enoch.)

> But as for the spirits of the Earth which were born upon the Earth, on the Earth shall be their dwelling. And the spirits of the giants afflict, oppress, destroy, attack, do battle, and work destruction on the earth, and cause trouble:

> they take no food, but nevertheless hunger and thirst, and cause offences. And these spirits shall rise up against the children of men and against the women, because they have proceeded from them.[124]

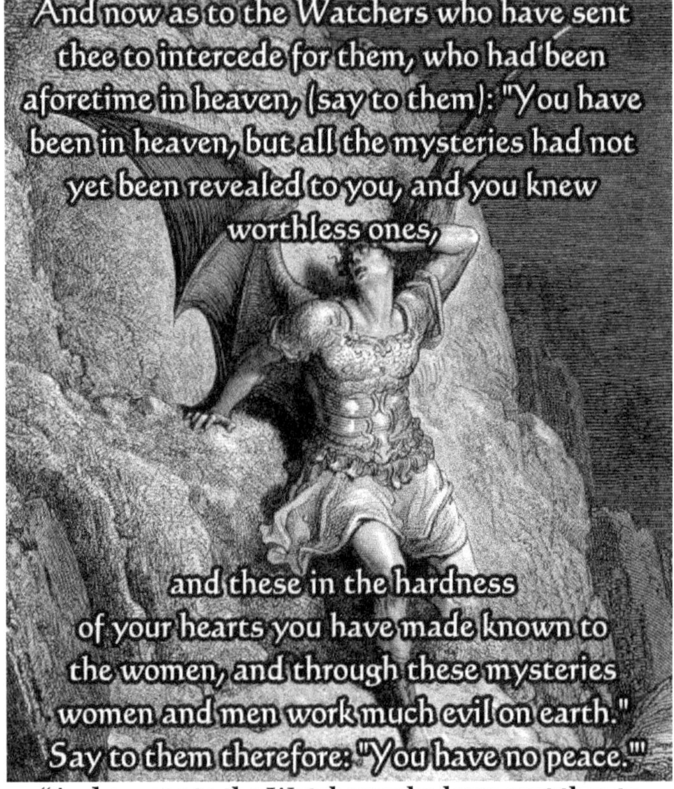

"And now as to the Watchers who have sent thee to intercede for them, who had been aforetime in heaven, say to them: 'You have been in heaven, but all the mysteries had not yet been revealed to you, and you knew worthless ones, and these in the hardness of your hearts you have made known to the women, and through these mysteries women and men work much evil on earth.' Say to them therefore: "You have no peace.'"
Public domain image of Satan, engraving by Gustave Dore, in John Milton's *Paradise Lost*

2. Greco-Roman mythology

In Greco-Roman mythology, when the Titans attacked and Jove defeated them with thunderbolts and flames, they fell to earth and their blood gave rise to the immoral race, just as the original ethereal energy gave rise to the men of the gold, silver, and bronze ages. Ovid's *Metamorphoses* includes an account of violent gods whose blood mixed with the earth and gave rise to a new race of violent men. (The endnote also sources the quote in the graphic.)

> ... They say that the Giants aspired to the sovereignty of Heaven, and piled the mountains, heaped together, even to the lofty stars. [58]

Then the omnipotent Father, hurling his lightnings, broke through Olympus, and struck Ossa away from Pelion, that lay beneath it.
Lightning over cliffs Stock-xchng,com jadegreen images

> While the dreadful carcasses lay overwhelmed beneath their own structure, they say that the Earth was wet, drenched with the plenteous blood of her sons, and that she gave life to the warm gore; and that, lest no memorial of this ruthless race should be surviving, she shaped them into the form of men. But that generation, too, was a despiser of the Gods above, and most greedy of ruthless slaughter, and full of violence: you might see that they derived their origin from blood.[58]

These descriptions echo the rebellious, violent nature of fallen angels and fallen man before the flood.

D. The Reason for Judgment

The Catholic Catechism discusses Original Sin[59] and includes this heritage of violence and wickedness.

> The harmony in which they had found themselves, thanks to original justice, is now destroyed: the control of the soul's spiritual faculties over the body is shattered; the union of man and woman becomes subject to tensions, their relations henceforth marked by lust and domination. Harmony with creation is broken: visible creation has become alien and hostile to man. Because of man, creation is now subject "to its bondage to decay." Finally, the consequence explicitly foretold for this disobedience will come true: man will "return to the ground," for out of it he was taken. Death makes its entrance into human history.
>
> After that first sin, the world is virtually inundated by sin. There is Cain's murder of his

> brother Abel and the universal corruption which follows in the wake of sin.[59]

Ye are of your father the devil,
and the lusts of your father ye will do.
He was a murderer
FROM THE BEGINNING,
and abode not in the truth, because
there is no truth in him. When he speaketh
a lie, he speaketh of his own: for he is a liar,
and the father of it. And because I tell you
the truth, ye believe me not.

"Ye are of your father the devil, and the lusts of your father ye will do. He was a murderer from the beginning, and abode not in the truth, because there is no truth in him. When he speaketh a lie, he speaketh of his own: for he is a liar, and the father of it. And because I tell you the truth, ye believe me not." (John 8:44-45), Dagger image Pubic Domain

Many of the teachings of Christ on Earth reinforced the authority of the Old Testament. Those who want to dismiss Genesis as allegory or myth are no different from Ovid or these other works we have quoted. They ignore the words of Christ. Jesus Christ said Moses wrote the truth. He didn't say that some of it was true and some of it was allegory, but that all of it was truth.

Christ also makes it clear that not only can our works not save us, but also that the origin of our reasoning has a corrupted source.

A favorite tactic of the skeptics and unbelievers of Jesus' day was to accuse Christ of being demon-possessed and of being a liar. They tried to discredit His authority for the things He said. They claimed to be "of God" when they were "of their father the Devil."

> *Which of you convinceth me of sin? And if I say the truth, why do ye not believe me? He that is of God heareth God's words: ye therefore hear them not, because ye are not of God. Then answered the Jews, and said unto him, Say we not well that thou art a Samaritan, and hast a devil? Jesus answered, I have not a devil; but I honour my Father, and ye do dishonour me. And I seek not mine own glory: there is one that seeketh and judgeth.* (John 8:44-50)

Summary and Chronology

XII. Summary and Chronology

Satan, like the rest of God's creation, began "very good", an angelic being of beauty and power. He fell through pride and desire to be "like the Most High". Other angelic beings joined him in rebellion. The world before the flood was corrupted by the person man chose as his father, Satan. Fallen angels may have helped Satan in his deception of man, perverting marriage and seducing and corrupting man morally and physically.

The serpent was a willing participant in the deception and fall, which unleashed lust on the world: pride, greed, and violence, as well as sexual sins. Psychotropic drugs may have had their beginning in the Tree of the Knowledge of Good and Evil and in the substances used both for worship and for personal adornment. God is not the author of evil, but He makes use for His judgments of the calamities that result.

Ancient records apart from the Bible echo its testimony to the increase of lust and violence. They also bear testimony to man's determination to blame the gods and to exalt himself as a god or the son of the gods. Even in ancient times man wanted to be "of his father the Devil" rather than submit to God, his true Creator. Man created "works salvation" and state religions to avoid submitting to the only true King and the Redeemer, Jesus Christ. Cain brought what he had made, the fruit of the ground, as an offering rather than what God required, and resorted to murder when rejected.

Cain and Seth both produced offspring but only Seth's line is recorded in the genealogies mentioned before the flood. Cain's descendant, Lamech, murdered without repentance.

As man's skills to create civilization grew he chose to mingle legitimate crafts with corrupted, occult knowledge taken from Satan and the fallen angels. He also justified himself by inventing gods and setting himself up to be divine ruler and priest, a practice that continued after the flood with Nimrod.

"Sons of God" can be interpreted differently but the Scriptures say their behavior led to greater corruption. They had descendants who were "mighty men", giants. Various ancient sources repeat the message of growing sinfulness often led by wicked "deities". Man continued to deceive himself and to be deceived by Satan but blamed unpredictable behavior by the "gods".

Jesus Christ testified to the authority of the Genesis record and His own authority and revealed the true source of unbelief as being the influence of Satan.

Chronology Before the Flood

(Does not include line of Cain)"
Adam (930 years) at 130 years became the father of
Seth (912 years) at 105 years became the father of
Enos (905 years) at 90 years became the father of
Cainan (910 years) at 70 years became the father of
Mahalaleel (895 years) at 65 years became the father of
Jared (962 years) at 162 years became the father of
Enoch (365 years)
("And Enoch walked with God: and he was not; for God

took him.") at 65 years became the father of
Methuselah (969 years) at 187 years became the father of
Lamech (777 years) at 182 years became the father of:
Noah
("This same shall comfort us concerning our work and toil of our hands, because of the ground which the LORD hath cursed")
lived 500 years before becoming father of Shem, Ham, and Japheth. (Graphic below is this data in chart form.)

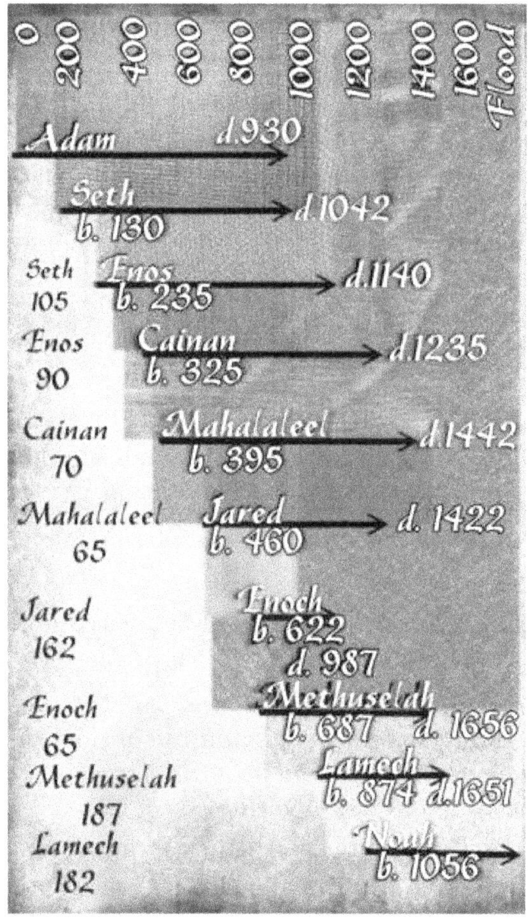

COA2 Review Questions

Some or all of these questions may be assigned. The questions to be used and the depth of the answers are entirely up to the teacher's discretion. Essay assignments can vary in length and research versus "thought" or "opinion" content should be balanced. More questions are included than are needed so that the teacher can pick and choose.

1. At the conclusion of creation, what statement does God make about it?

Everything was very good.

2. What is described in two different states in the Scripture passages from Ezekiel and Isaiah?

Satan in his original state as a cherub and later in his fallen state.

3. List three things we know about Satan's condition before his rebellion.

a. Cherub b. adorned with gold and jewels c. walked in Eden. d. walked on the holy mountain of God (or among the fiery stones) e. wise and beautiful f. seal of perfection g. blameless in his ways

4. List three things we know about Satan's condition after his rebellion

a. filled with violence b.expelled from among the fiery stones c. proud heart d. corrupted wisdom e. driven out in disgrace f. desired to be like the Most High g. destined for sheol/the pit h. took a third of the angels along in his rebellion

5. Make two comparisons between Satan's rebellion in Scripture and the "sin of Zu", likenesses or differences

Likenesses: a. desire for majesty in his heart b. seeking a throne c. ruling angels d. warring against God

Differences a. fleeing b. hiding

6. Write a brief report researching demons, "sons of God" and/or fallen angels. Explain different theories about the nature of these beings and use Sripture quotes to support the statement in the text "Whatever their origins, the Scriptures teach that there are myriads of evil spirits."

Answers may vary and the teacher may divide up or limit the focus of the report based on the needs of the students. Remind students that most of what is said about demons is not certain, but that they may refer to the information in the text to answer the question. The student should include references to the instances of demon possession in the New Testament, the theories about the nature of the "sons of God", legitimate sources that discuss the Nephilim (there are many wild, unsubstantiated theories that have no evidence but are very popular) and any Old Testament evidences of Satan's activities before the flood.

7. How does Satan's authority over his fallen angels differ from that of sovereign kings and rulers?

He is a chosen leader of a group of relative equals and must keep control by force

8. Give one possible interpretation of the Epic of Atrahasis if it refers to Satan's relationship with other fallen angels.

Answers may vary but may include that Satan has to deal with unrest, but he and other angels are not weak and should not be underestimated.

9. Explain the meaning of Satan's name "the busy one".

He is constantly going around the earth (seeking his own advancement and man's corruption) and is too busy to submit to God

10. Write a brief essay explaining where and with whom sin originated. Include Scriptures and outside sources that support the answer.

Sin originated with Satan, in the spiritual realm. Scriptures state that sin did not originate with God (several are included in this text) and also that sin did not affect the material world as a direct result of Satan's rebellion. Student should remember that Satan entered the Garden of Eden to tempt man while creation was still "very good" and man was still innocent. The ability of man to talk to animals, to walk with God, to eat from the Tree of Life are all implied or clearly indicated in Scripture. After man's fall, sin crossed over from the spiritual to the material universe. Death, separation from God, inability to speak to animals, need for sacrifices, and the specifics of the curse outlined by God upon Adam, Eve, and the Serpent are all evidences of sin's effects on the material universe, but Satan liar, tempter, destroyer was active before the fall of man.

11. What is the right answer to the question of why God created Satan?

Deuteronomy 29:29

12. What foundation and standard did Adam set up before the fall?

Marriage

13. How did Satan corrupt marriage to make Adam fall?

Answers may vary but Satan deceived Eve, forcing Adam to choose between her and God and successfully tempting him to eat the fruit as well because of his love for Eve.

14. What are two questions arising from the serpent's behavior?

a. How could it decide to do evil? b. What kind of reptile was it? c. Was animal speech with humans normal before the fall?

15. Chose one of the three questions about the serpent asked in the text of the book and write a brief essay, supporting your position on the answer to the question with Scripture and at least one other outside source.

Answers may vary but should include reference to material covered in the text as part of the response. Josephus' Antiquities is a good source for more detailed information based on Jewish scholarship. Students may wish to find instances of humans speaking to animals in other ancient sources but it is difficult to use examples that fit the context of the prefall condition or give any time reference or special condition of man enabling him to understand them that fits this discussion.

16. What promise is included in the punishments God lists after the fall?

The Redeemer

17. Write a brief essay commenting on the discussion in the text about Adam and Eve's "eyes being opened" and the knowledge of their nakedness. You may choose to discuss shame, lust, the play on words as exemplified by

"nude" and "shrewd", the evidence for the presence of angels, or another topic approved by the teacher. Include scriptural support and two outside sources.

Answers will vary but students should support their conclusions with research in the Scriptures and outside sources. Discussion of shame could include the commentary on the Hebrews passage. Students might give other examples of the use of "play on words" images in the Bible. Caution students about the topic of angels being present in the Garden because heresies associated with the theories about the nature of the fall and angels' part in it abound.

18. Research the topic of psychotropic drug use in religious practices. Include reference and possible explanations for God calling sacrifices and incense offerings "a sweet savour" in the Old Testament. Consult external sources and mention at least three different religions. Note that even some Christian churches use incense in their services. Comment on Adam's offering from the Book of Jubilees and its possible significance. This assignment will involve jumping to several different parts of the text. The student might most easily find these various topics by starting in the appendix.

This is an optional research assignment. and answers will vary. The teacher should caution the student against delving into any kind of concentrated study of false religions or detailed accounts of drug use and the effects. The purpose of this assignment is to make students aware of the good side of worship aided by natural substances and also to warn against the deceptive practices of those who seek a "natural high" or "spiritual awakening" and the dangers of these practices. Students should consider the statement in the text that these natural substances can still be used to weaken mental and physical defenses and help human and spiritual forces gain control over subjects who surrender their wills to these "worship practices".

19. Why was Cain so afraid of a death sentence resulting from his murder of Abel if God did not intend to kill him?

He feared his own relatives or the animals might kill him, or that he would starve to death if the ground failed to yield enough food for him.

20. Give evidence that Cain may have repented.

a. "From thy face shall I be hid" implies that he would regret separation from God. b. Naming his son and city "Enoch", when Enoch means "consecration", hints that he may have consecrated his son and his efforts at city-building to God as an act of repentance.

21. What was the apparent difference between Lamech's act of murder and Cain's?

Lamech seemed defiant and Cain seemed repentant.

22. Briefly compare and contrast the arts and crafts begun by Lamech's sons and the knowledge imparted to the "daughters of men" by the "sons of God".

Lamechs sons created and developed good, legitimate, needed skills and desirable inventions. The "sons of god" gave occult and corrupting knowledge that did not benefit man, since there were already legitimate ways of acquiring knowledge and skill with natural substances and metalworking, for example.

23. Give one example of how the Epic of Atrahasis quote parallels the biblical account of Noah.

Noah had influence with the men of his day ("preacher of righteousness" implies that some at least listened to him speak). But he held different beliefs from the other men of his day and was shunned or made to dwell apart from them "They have expelled me from the land. Since

I have always reverenced Enki," and that Noah alone was "found righteous".

24. Briefly summarize Dr. David Livingston's observations about world myths and legends.

They were created to support the king and the priesthood in controlling the population, and have no real substance as beliefs that people really held. The people were taught these "beliefs" in public ceremonies and readings of the "laws", a counterfeit of the reading of God's true law by priests and scribes. Rulers could claim to be the descendant of a god, confiscate property, demand enslavement, raise armies, and do anything they desired based on the teaching of the religion supported by the invented priesthood. This is where the false church-state union began, and it has always been a means for man to exalt himself.

25. Write a brief essay to summarize man-based and works-based religions, mentioning at least two of the religions from the text and giving specifics.

Yoruba teaches that a godlike leader left the people without knowledge of how to please the gods and the flood was a punishment for their ignorance. Confucianism claims that making this life good is all that matters. Hinduism mingles spiritual success with material and demands study, good deeds, and oddly mixes responsibility with sensual pleasure. Buddhism is very similar to Hinduism in its emphasis on minimizing discomfort and maximizing self-fulfillment. Roman Catholic church teaches baptism, among other things, as required for salvation. Islam has many rules and Mohammed himself had no assurance of heaven but demanded obedience and taught that hearts would be weighed and good and bad deeds balanced against each other.

26. Give two examples from ancient records of the increase of evil and violence in the Earth.

a. 200 Angels in Book of Enoch *thought they would escape punishment by taking human wives. b. Zu forcibly took a wife (possibly a human woman) and seduced and corrupted her with perfumes and jewels c. Zoroastrian Epic records jealousy and violence in the enemy of the king d. Book of Jubilees records "sons of God" wickedness and how evil grew e. Zadokite Document records lust of "watchers" and fall of "strong heroes"*

27. Write an essay comparing the modern indifference to sins such as adultery, abortion, prostitution, homosexuality to the excuses people made by worshiping gods like Xochipilli, Kurupi, Kamaveda and Freyr.

This is a "thought" question so answers will vary but students might research excuses people today give to justify sin. It is not recommended that they do much research into these gods, since their descriptions and actions are for the most part extremely evil and disgusting. The point of the exercise is to get the students to realize that from ancient times man has excused his sin. The excuses have simply changed form. Man has always said that some force beyond his control made him sin. He refuses to acknowledge God's power to change desires and behavior.

28. How does Socrates define demons and heroes?

Demons are wise "golden" advisors and heroes are the offspring of divine beings (implying that they could be descended from these "demons".

29. How does Ovid contrast gods and men in his creation story?

Gods can be unpredictable and violent but man is a glorious creation with divine greatness.

30. The Watchers in the *Book of Enoch* and the "blood-born" descendants of the Titans and the legacy retold in the Catholic Catechism have what in common?

"No peace", violence, death, corruption.

31. Name two truths about the Scriptures that Christ reinforces.

a. Genesis is divinely inspired and authoritative. b. Satan is the father of lies, lust, and all sin c. He was obedient to the commands of Scripture, demonstrating their authority, in contrast to the hypocrisy and pride of the teachers of the Law

COA2 Vocabulary

1. describe

"At some point God created the being described below."

using a list of characteristics of something to make its appearance, nature, or functions clear

2. Blameless

"*You were blameless in your ways from the day you were created ...*"

without sin or guilt

3. wickedness (context sentence follows number 7 below)

4. widespread

5. expelled

6. corrupt

7. splendor

"*... till wickedness was found in you. Through your widespread trade you were filled with violence, and you sinned. So I drove you in disgrace from the mount of God, and I expelled you, guardian cherub, from among the fiery stones. Your heart became proud on account of your beauty, and you corrupted your wisdom because of your splendor.*"

Wickedness: practicing evil as part of one's nature

Widespread: covering extensive territory

Expelled: thrown out with no prospect of return; banished

Corrupt: marked by immorality and perversion; depraved

Splendor: brilliance, magnificence, grandeur

8. ascend (context sentence follows number 10 below)

9. exalt

10. congregation

For thou hast said in thine heart, I will ascend into heaven, I will exalt my throne above the stars of God: I will sit also upon the mount of the congregation, the sides of the north: I will ascend above the clouds; I will be like the most High.

Ascend: mount up; go to a higher place, such as Heaven

Exalt: lift up; give praise and honor to

Congregation: assembly of people for the purpose of worship

11. recesses (context sentence follows number 12 below)

12. ponder

"Nevertheless, you will be thrust down to Sheol, to the recesses of the pit. Those who see you will gaze at you, they will ponder over you, saying, 'Is this the man who made the earth tremble, who shook kingdoms, who made the world like a wilderness and overthrew its cities, who did not allow his prisoners to go home?"

Recesses: deepest, most hidden or out of the way places

Ponder: seriously consider; think deeply about

13. adorn

“He walked in stones of fire (probably volcanic activity), and was adorned in gold and jewels.”

decorate with; enhance beauty with ornaments

14. deceive (context sentence follows number 15 below)

15. rebel

“Though we have no time reference, at some time Satan deceived a third of the angels into joining him in rebelling against God.”

Deceive: lie to; practice falsehood upon

Rebel: to resist or defy an authority or a generally accepted convention

16. cuneiform

“The cuneiform tablets of the Assyrian people are among the oldest surviving documents in the world.”

ancient wedge-shaped characters formed in clay tablets and supplying the alphabet for many ancient languages

17. myriads

“Whatever their origins, the Scriptures teach that there are myriads of evil spirits.”

huge numbers; so many as to be impossible to determine or define the quantity

18. realm

“So even though the entire realm of rebellious angels, demons and unclean spirits united in rebellion against God, they are only kept in line by force.”

a field, sphere, or province

19. beneficial (context sentence follows number 20 below)

20. parallels

"Still, it is beneficial to examine parallels in other ancient documents, especially those which claim to be a record of times before the flood."

Beneficial: good; helpful; having advantages

Parallels: accounts having common or similar features

21. industry

"Satan's answer, *From going to and fro in the earth, and from walking up and down in it* shows Satan's industry."

showing energy and enthusiasm; being busy and active about a task

22. banishment

"This passage in Revelation describes the banishment from heaven of Satan and his angels."

cast out from a place and forbidden to return

23. achievement

"After his own fall, it appears that the first step Satan took to again attempt to 'be like the Most High' was to corrupt God's crowning achievement, the being created to worship God and to fellowship with Him: man."

result of great skill and effort; an accomplishment

24. accuser (context sentence follows number 25 below)

25. fondness

"Satan is also known as the accuser, because of his fondness for pointing out man's sin, the sin he led man into."

Accuser: someone who points out another's wrong acts or sins

Fondness: being pleased by or liking something

26. association

"Note also, here and in other ancient texts, that changing into animal or part-animal forms appear in close association with sin and rebellion."

connections or relationships between things

27. assume

"This is important to remember, whether Satan actually assumed the form of the serpent, or even if he only indwelt the serpent or controlled its actions."

to take on a different appearance; to change into

28. resolution

"6. From the will of his heart a resolution he did ...
7. In his own heart a resolution he made,"

firm intention or decision to do something

29. intend (context sentence follows number 31 below)

30. obsess

31. exhaustive

"He did not intend for us to be obsessed with evil, to exhaustively study it. He intended for the brief scriptural mentions of evil to be enough to keep us from it."

Intend: having a purpose or reason for doing something

Obsess: constantly think about something and make most actions revolve around that idea

Exhaustive: covering every possible thought, idea, or piece of information about a subject

32. fragment

"The other ancient texts quoted here are simply further evidence that man once knew the truth and still had fragments of it in his memories, even as he wrote his own ideas and imaginings and invented his own religions."

very small portion remaining from a whole that is lost or forgotten

33. condemn

"Jesus quoted Adam's 'wedding vows' when He condemned divorce, giving this statement the authority of God."

state that something is wrong and forbid its practice

34. regenerate

"Removed skillfully and carefully, certain rib tissue will regenerate, even today. "

grow back; remake lost parts

35. ridicule

"The concept of *one flesh* is ridiculed by Secular Humanists today, and Satan attacked marriage from the beginning."

mocked or made fun of

36. *motif*

"This tactic is so well known that it is a common *motif* through much of the world's literature."

dominant theme or central idea; recurring element

37. especially

"Though it seems to have been made especially for man, many creatures besides Adam and Eve lived in that garden, and one of them was the serpent."

tailored or custom-created for a particular purpose

38. subtle

> *"Now the serpent was more subtle than any beast of the field which the LORD God had made* (Genesis 3:1a KJV).

"Subtle means crafty, sneaky, clever at doing things you really should not be doing."

the word is defined in the text

39. characteristics

"From the very beginning different types of animals had different characteristics."

distinguishing features; things that make a creature different form other creatures

40. fable (context sentence follows number 41 below)

41. allegory

"But this is not one of Aesop's fables or just an allegory."

Fable: a story, usually short; with a single, specific lesson or moral to teach

Allegory: an extended story using physical or concrete things to teach spiritual lessons. Pilgrim's Progress *teaches the various aspects of a person's sinful state, dawning awareness of the need for salvation, experience of conversion, and events related to Christian life, growth, and/or service.*

42. conversation

"Third, since the serpent carried on a conversation, first with Eve, then with the LORD, was this something unusual, even a miracle, or was this common?"

speech back and forth between two or more parties with the goal of mutual understanding

43. descendant

"All snakes which crawl on their bellies are genetic descendants of this serpent."

born from the direct genetic line of

44. instance

"There is only one other instance in the Bible of an animal speaking."

occurrence; happening

45. accustomed

"Have I ever been accustomed to do so to you?"

made a habit of; practiced or did as a regular action

46. mimic

"Nor are these like modern animals, such as parrots and myna birds mimicking human speech without understanding."

imitate or duplicate sounds

47. volition

"Because God judged the serpent, it seems that the serpent had both intellect and volition."

ability to make choices; freedom to make decisions or take actions

48. disposition (context sentence follows number 49 below)

49. envious

"... all the living creatures had one language, at that time the serpent, which then lived together with Adam and his wife, shewed an envious disposition ..."

Disposition: general behavior or mood; usual emotions or responses

Envious: wanting what another has; desiring things

possessed by someone else

50. distinction

"Just after Creation, God records an observation about Adam and Eve that, to a twenty-first century westerner, seems to be the strangest statement to show the distinction between man in his state of innocence and the difference after the fall of the human race."

showing how two things are different; clarifying a "before and after" state

51. disclaimer

"... Secular Humanist cannot allow the smallest seed of truth, they added the following disclaimer. This disclaimer, quoted below, is now included in the description at the British Museum exhibit."

explanation that denies responsibility or connection with something (In the case of the example in the text, the museum gives an item's name when it was discovered but claims it has become convinced that the name is not accurate.)

52. scenario

"A century later, museum scholars determined it to be one of a well-known class of mythic scenarios featuring one of the earliest historical images of the Tree Of Life, timeless Mesopotamian symbol of earthly creation."

a set of circumstances or actions described or illustrated

53. abstain (context sentence follows number 54 below)

54. destruction

"God therefore commanded that Adam and his wife should eat of all the rest of the plants, but to abstain from the Tree of Knowledge; and foretold to them, that if they touched it, it would prove their destruction."

Abstain: avoid doing something

Destruction: ruin, spoil, tear apart, demolish

55. develop

"That made the Tree of the Knowledge of Good and Evil a necessary test. God was developing moral character."

seeking to encourage growth

56. atonement (context sentence follows number 57 below)

57. resurrection

"If there was no sin causing a Fall and the Universe is not under a curse, there is no need for an atonement, no need for a sinless savior, no need for the Law or the resurrection."

Atonement: redemption from sin by the sacrifice of Christ

Resurrection: return to life from the dead

58. candid (context sentence follows number 59 below)

59. unembellished

"The serpent was crafty in the sense of *candid*. We use the words 'naked' or 'candid' the same way today, as in 'the naked truth,' meaning complete and unembellished."

Candid: completely honest

Unembellished: without unnecessary details or added material

60. implication (context sentence follows number 62 below)

61. exposed

62. humiliate

"Hebrews 10:33 discusses the implications of being exposed and humiliated."

Exposed: subjected to public view without possibility of concealment; revealed or made bare

Humiliate: to cause shame, disgrace, or loss of status

63. psychotropic

Graham Hancock, in his book *Supernatural: Meetings with the Ancient Teachers of Mankind,* he believes that the fruit Adam and Eve ate *"sharpened their understanding"* (Josephus) through a psychotropic effect.

affecting thought or mental processes; also thought to give spiritual insight

64. anthropological

"There is an anthropological and archaeological theory ... that seems to offer at least a partial answer to this question"

the study of man's cultural development

65. necromancer

There shall not be found among you any one that maketh his son or his daughter to pass through the fire, or that useth divination, or an observer of times, or an enchanter, or a witch, or a charmer, or a consulter with familiar spirits, or a wizard, or a necromancer.

communicating with the dead to tell the future

66. whirlwind

"As I looked, and behold, a whirlwind came out of the north"

Storm of wind moving in a circular fashion; tornado or cyclone

67. transacted

"All who are in the heavens know what is transacted there ... without transgressing the commands, which they have received."

things that are carried out or accomplished

68. motive (context sentence follows number 70 below)

69. prohibition

70. ascribe

"The motive ascribed as underlying the prohibition against sin is the benefit of man."

Motive: purpose in doing something

Prohibition: forbidding something

Ascribe: attribute something to a certain cause

71. perversion (context sentence follows number 73 below)

72. distortion

73. communal

"Sin defiles the body and corrupts the mind; it is a perversion and distortion of the principles of nature; it creates disorder and confusion in society; it brings mischief, misery, and trouble into communal life ... "

Perversion: corrupting something from its original form or purpose

Distortion: warped or twisted from its prper form

Communal: living together; sharing habitation or resources

74. commendable

"Stealing another tribe's horses, for example, is considered highly commendable."

worthy of praise

75. guideline (context sentence follows number 76 below)

76. parameter

"The curse sets the guidelines or parameters for all of human history."

Guidelines: rules for actions

Parameters: limits to be kept within

77. sacrifice

"The first sacrifice was offered before the birth of Seth, but after enough time had passed that Cain (a tiller of the ground) and his younger brother Abel (a keeper of the flocks) were old enough to be working on their own."

Offering to God made with the right heart attitude toward Him and following set practices according to commandments from Him

78. presuppose

"As Keil and Delitzsch said, 'we must bear in mind that the first sacrifices wcording to ere offered after the fall, and therefore presupposed the spiritual separation of man from God, and were designed to satisfy the need of the heart for fellowship with God'."

Accepted as an existing condition; took into account as a true circumstance

79. opportunity

"When God came to Cain, He first gave him the opportunity to repent by asking him where his brother Abel was."

chance to accomplish a needed purpose

80. pronounce (context sentence follows number 81 below)

81. immediate

"He pronounced immediate judgment."

state what is to happen with authority and certainty

Immediate: to happen at once; without delay

82. vagrant

"The ground *'will no longer yield its strength to you; you will be a vagrant and a wanderer on the earth'.*"

wanderer; person with no fixed residence

83. consequences

"Ussher points out part of what Cain had to fear as consequences of murdering his brother."

results of actions

84. conscience

"'Cain might justly fear, through the conscience of his crime, that every man that met him would also slay him'."

In this context (a quotation from an older source with a nonstandard use of the word), the word means the same as consciousness, or the understanding and knowledge that wrongdoing has taken place.

85. cultivation

"It says the ground *"no longer yielded its strength,"* meaning cultivation and farming would require much more work."

To improve and prepare (land), as by plowing or fertilizing, for raising crops; till.

86. specialization

"It does mean people living close together with specialization of labor."

dividing responsibilities into particular types of work as opposed to general labor

87. fusible

The classical Greek culture said that blacksmiths worked with "fusibles."

metal forged by melting, heating, and combining

88. permission

"Since tents were made out of leather and God had not yet given permission to eat meat, Jabal founded the leather industry."

allowed or extended the right to do something

89. repentance

"Lamech's 'sword song' shows the anger of his great-great-great grandfather Cain when he killed his brother Abel, but no evidence of repentance."

acknowledging guilt for sin and turning away from it

90. polygamy

Whatever the reason, Lamech brags to his wives (he is also the first polygamist) that he has murdered "a young man."

marrying multiple spouses

91. kernel

"The following explains why we do not 'support' or 'prop up' the accuracy of the Scriptures with other ancient works, but only cite them when they agree with and contain kernels of the same the truth already expressed in the something Bible."

small, essential part of something

92. fabricate

"The myths and epics of the ancient near east are fabricated religio-politico documents with a calculated purpose."

create something that is not authentic in a historic or cultural sense but is presented as such to mislead or outright deceive

93. enunciate

"The goal of the myth, progressively more clearly enunciated in time, has become the destruction of history and the enthronement of man as the new governor of the universe."

gradually made clear by the evidence found in statements pronouncements

94. ambitious (context sentence follows number 96 below)

95. voluptuous

96. degenerate

"Thus, one should see the myths and epics for what they are: a deliberate attempt by ambitious and evil men (under the leadership of evil spiritual influences) to subjugate the populace and extort from them, along with the supporting priest-nobles, all that is needed for the most voluptuous lifestyle. When man becomes completely degenerate, he will develop a system to support his degeneracy."

Ambitious: desiring more and more power, influence, or control

Voluptuous:- rich, sensual, opulent

Degenerate: corrupt; given over to selfish and wicked desires

97. lenient (context sentence follows number 98 below)

98. relinquish

"Occasionally a ruler might be more lenient with the people. But, none ever relinquishes divine kingship."

Lenient: allowing more freedom or being more gracious or merciful

Relinquish: give up or cease to expect something

99. achievements

"Confucianism is one of the best and easiest to understand examples of a man-made religion that exalts man's earthly efforts and achievements, and the supposed 'unknowable' nature of god and heaven."

things accomplished that are worthy of praise or commendation

100. concentrate (context sentence follows number 101 below)

101. appropriate

"[It] concentrates on appropriate behavior in life, not a future heaven."

Concentrate: focus on; present as central or most important

Appropriate: correct or right

102. ancestors

"The afterlife is unknowable, so all effort should be made to make this life the best it can be, to honor ancestors, and to respect elders."

people you are descended from

103. prescribe

"Three ways have been prescribed by which one may attain perfection, or be liberated from the bondage of Samsara."

to establish rules, laws, or directions

104. contention

"Hindu writings are very difficult to understand but, in spite of the contention below that 'Moksha' (the chief goal of life) cannot be 'produced', clearly works are necessary to achieve these goals."

insistence that something is true

105. constitutes

"... a clear doctrine of salvation in the Buddha's teachings: Salvation in early Buddhism was nirvana, the extinguishing of the all karma that constitutes the self."

that which makes up something; its essence or composition

106. alleviation

The Buddha said little about nirvana, because he felt that the alleviation of suffering was far more important

making less severe or burdensome; improving conditions for

107. attachments

"... focusing on the goal of ultimate salvation would only lead to more attachments, and therefore more suffering."

connections or things that tie a person to someone or something else

108. encourage

"Rather than focus on nirvana as a goal, therefore, lay Buddhists were encouraged to give donations of goods, services, or money to monks or monasteries; to chant or copy sutras; and to engage in other activities in order to gain merit that could lead to a more desirable rebirth, which would bring them closer to enlightenment."

prompt or try to persuade people to do something

109. contrite

"Paradise be brought near unto the Pious: 'This is what ye have been promised: to every one who hath turned in penitence to God and kept his laws; Who hath feared the God of Mercy in secret, and come to him with a contrite heart: Enter it in peace: this is the day of Eternity'."

sorry for wrongdoing

110. heritage (context sentence follows number 111 below)

111. recompense

"This is Paradise, which ye have received as your heritage in recompense for your works;"

Heritage: enduring legacy; inheritance

Recompense: earned as a reward or payment

112. capricious

"The politically-created false gods are capricious, not to be relied on, but worshiped out of fear."

unpredictable; changing expectations or reactions

113. inflict (context sentence follows number 114 below)

114. rebuffed

"They inflict punishments when outwitted or when their lustful desires are rebuffed."

Inflict: subject to; direct at; impose on

Rebuff: reject; refuse to cooperate

115. seduce

"These repeated tales of gods seducing or trying to seduce mortals echo the lust of the sons of God in Genesis or the fallen angels of Enoch."

tempt to immorality or sexual wrongdoing

116. destined

"They certainly are sinful in that they rebelled with Satan and left their first estate and are destined for the Lake of Fire."

inevitable or necessary end result of previous actions r decisions

117. confirmed

"They all are confirmed in their personal choice."

determined; set on a course or action

118. transform

"It is for Adam's race who passed on his sin nature that Jesus died to forgive and transform."

change completely; remake as a new being

119. seminal p 56

"The problem I have with FALLEN angels cohabiting with women and having children is that the Bible clearly states our sin nature is passed down through Adam and his seminal descendants."

by transfer of semen from male to female; directly from genetic material supplied by a male through intercourse

120. accountable

"Mankind from Adam on are held accountable for their sin nature and sin (Rom 5:12ff), not fallen angels."

responsible; required to answer for actions and deal with consequences of decisions

121. justification

"I know what others teach on this. But I do not see any justification in Scripture for the fallen angel view."

support for or evidence to confirm correctness or truth

122. reconcile

"I cannot reconcile it with the Scripture's teaching on man's sinfulness or the doctrine of the Virgin Birth of Jesus Christ which rests on the fact that Jesus had no sinful nature because the seed of His conception was from the Holy Spirit not man."

compare two things and conclude they do not contradict or negate each others' possibility

123. counterfeit

"So the counterfeits invented by 'divine rulers' would ring true in the minds of those distant from the source of truth."

false, but made to closely imitate and pass for an original, true thing

124. overthrow

"It describes how early man grew in knowledge, technology, and prosperity, but also records the attacks of the evil enemy seeking to overthrow him."

conquer, remove from power, destroy or enslave

125. epic

"The epic records how magical beings and even beasts were used in this battle, hinting at the spiritual and physical aspects of man's early history on Earth."

story about heroic deeds of natural and supernatural beings that is grand in scope both in a physical and spiritual sense

126. nurture

"He took up his abode in the mountains, ... from him sprang all kindly nurture and the arts of clothing, till then unknown."

helping something to grow and thrive in all ways, physical and mental/spiritual

127. homage

"Men and beasts from all parts of the earth came to do him homage and receive laws at his hands, and his glory was like to the sun."

respect, reverence, admiration, tribute, submission

128. waxed

"Then Ahriman the Evil, when he saw how the Shah's honour was increased, waxed envious, and sought to usurp the diadem of the world."

grew; became and increased in degree

129. version

"The *Book of Jubilees* records its version of the sins of man that led up to the flood."

a variation or different example of something

130. commandment (context sentence follows number 131 below)

131. kindle

"These became as though they had never been, because they did their own pleasure and kept not the commandments of their Maker. In the end His anger was kindled against them."

Commandment: one of the orders, rules, or laws a ruler gives his people for their good

Kindle: start; cause to produce

132. cultures

"Cultures around the world worshiped gods who had sexual relationships with humans."

groups of people sharing similar or related practices and beliefs

133. mischief

"And mighty marks of mischief leave behind;"

physical or psychological activity with the intention of interrupting or upsetting normal routines or activity and sometimes doing serious harm or damage

134. remnants

"Pleas'd with the remnants of departing light"

leftovers; remaining parts

135. frowning

"While frowning Auster seeks the Southern sphere;"

facial expression indicating anger, displeasure, or disapproval

136. reassures (context sentence follows number 137 below)

137. essence

"But Ovid reassures the reader that a 'better' creation is coming, and that man's essence includes divine..."

Reassures: comforts with the idea of a satisfactory resolution of conflict or uncertainties

Essence: most basic, real, and unchanging part of something

138. perverted

"This truth is perverted all around the world in myths that claim the divine creative energy actually makes man have the nature of a god."

corrupted; lied about; misrepresented

139. erected (context sentence follows number 140 below)

140. hereditary

"Man looks aloft; and with erected eyes Beholds his own hereditary skies."

erected (this is an archaic meaning peculiar to this quote): lifted up; pointed heavenward

Hereditary: birthright; the place he will inherit; his rightful destination

141. metamorphosed

"From such rude principles our form began; And earth was metamorphos'd into Man."

changed from one form or nature to a different one

142. license

"In the Greco-Roman flood legends, Jove (Greek Zeus) felt justified in destroying the world because the text doesn't mention sexual license as being immorality."

belief that there are no consequences or responsibility for actions

143. obsession

"Sexual obsession is a very early form of immortality..."

unable to stop thinking about, pursuing, or trying to do something

144. constraints

"They were encouraged to transcend the natural world, to 'ascend,' part of the quest to evolve, to go beyond traditional moral constraints."

restrictions, limitations, or things that hold back from progress

145. excessive (context sentence follows number 146 below)

146. ornamentation

"Extreme and wrong desires or lusts resulted in warfare, misuse of metallurgy and weapons technology, excessive ornamentation and makeup."

Excessive: overdone; too much; far more than necessary

Ornamentation: decorations; jewelry

147. emetic

"It can have poisonous properties similar to arsenic, causing liver damage, and also may have emetic properties."

causing vomiting

148. exposure

"Excessive exposure can cause loss of mental clarity as well as serious health problems."

in close or frequent contact with something

149. dependency

"It may have been one of the ancient drugs used by Satan or his human agents to control the populace and to create dependency."

need for something; convinced something is necessary to success, well-being, or survival

150. occult

"He sought and was given occult knowledge that was bad for him and led him into sin."

spiritual power from an evil source

151. intercede

"The condemned watchers of the *Book of Enoch* ask him to intercede for them and he has a vision of taking their petition to God. God says they should intercede for men, not men for them."

act as a go-between asking for favor, help, or provision

152. ethereal

" ... They fell to earth and their blood gave rise to the immoral race, just as the original ethereal energy gave rise to the men of the gold silver and bronze ages."

spiritual, non-human, or godlike in origin

153. explicitly

"Finally, the consequence explicitly foretold for this disobedience will come true: man will 'return to the ground,' for out of it he was taken.

made very clear and plain; told without possibility of misunderstanding

154. inundated

"After that first sin, the world is virtually inundated by sin."

flooded, overwhelmed, immersed

155. reinforced

"Many of the teachings of Christ on Earth reinforced the authority of the Old Testament."

added authority to and made stronger

156. participant

"The serpent was a willing participant in the deception and fall, which unleashed lust on the world … "

cooperating with and playing a voluntary part in

157. determination

"They also bear testimony to man's determination to blame the gods and to exalt himself as a god or the son of the gods."

Decision to do something; mindset demanding that certain actions be taken or tasks accomplished

References, Footnotes, Expanded Study, and Appendix Materials

References, Footnotes, Expanded Study, and Appendix Materials

A. References to Outside Sources

1 *The Chaldean Account of Genesis,* by George Smith, (1876), From the Internet Sacred Text Archive, managed by John Bruno Hare. at sacred-texts.com http://www.sacred-texts.com/ane/caog/

George Smith (1840-1876) was an English Assyrologist, apprentice engraver, but self-taught in cuneiform in the corridors of the British Museum. Eventually he was hired by Sir Henry Rawlinson, prominent archaeologist. Smith achieved world-wide attention when he discovered an account of the flood with obvious Biblical parallels in 1872, related in *The Chaldean Account of the Deluge*. This book expands on the previous work, and presents numerous translations of tablets, including the first print appearance of the Gilgamesh (Idzubar) cycle. Some of the most important texts, such as the Descent of Ishtar and the account of the Flood are fairly intact, while others are in pieces. J.B. Hare, Dec. 15th, 2009.

CHAPTER VII. THE SIN OF THE GOD ZU. "This legend stands alone among the stories, its incidents and its principal actor being otherwise almost unknown from cuneiform sources. I have at present only detected one copy of the story, and this is in so mutilated a condition that it cannot be connected with any other of the legends. From some similarity in style, I conjecture that it may form the first tablet of the series which I have termed the 'Wars of the Gods'. I have, however, no sufficient evidence to connect the two, and for this reason give it here a separate place, preceding the tablets of the 'Wars of the Gods'.

"The principal actor in the legend is a being named Zu, the name being found in all three cases of an Assyrian noun Zu, Za and Zi. Preceding the name is the determinative of divinity, from which I judge Zu to have been ranked among the gods."

2 *Epic of Atrahasis: Myths from Mesopotamia: Creation, the Flood, Gilgamesh, and Others* (Oxford World's Classics) [Paperback] Stephanie Dalley translator Publisher: Oxford University Press, USA (September 17, 1998). From the Internet Sacred Text Archive, managed by John Bruno Hare.

3 *The Chaldean Account of Genesis*.

4 Rib regeneration Munro IR, Guyuron B (November 1981). "Split-Rib Cranioplasty". *Annals of Plastic Surgery* 7 (5): 341-346. http://www.ncbi.nlm.nih.gov/pubmed/7332200 (Skull repair was successfully accomplished using rib graft. The rib portions removed completely regenerated.

5 Cassandra
http://www.theoi.com/Text/Apollodorus3.html

Accounts of Cassandra's gift of prophecy vary. Some say, as in the linked site above, that it was simply given as a gift. Others say she obtained it by spending the night in Apollo's temple and having his sacred snakes clean her ears so that she could hear the future. The following link tells about Tiresias, another prophet in Greek mythology, and how Athena cleaned his ears so he could hear the knowledge about the future in the songs of birds. Note that the story of Tiresias contains many strange and unpleasant variations and the teacher may want to restrict student access to the details. This link is provided only to support the Cassandra legend.

Note that "the Theoi Classical E-Texts Library is a collection of works from ancient Greek and Roman literature in translation. The theme of the library is classical mythology and so the selection presented consists primarily of ancient poetry (epic, lyric, bucolic, et. al.), drama and prose renditions of myth." http://www.library.theoi.com/

6 *The Orthodox Jewish Bible*, completed by Phillip Goble in 2002, is an English language version that applies Yiddish and Hasidic cultural expressions to the Messianic Bible. Copyright Information: The Orthodox Jewish Bible fourth edition, OJB. Copyright 2002,2003,2008,2010, 2011 by Artists for Israel International. All rights reserved. http://www.biblegateway.com/versions/Orthodox-Jewish-Bible-OJB/

7 Flavius Josephus, The Antiquities of the Jews, 93 AD, Translator: William Whiston, 1737.

8 Flavius Josephus.

9 *The Annals of the World* "The Origin of Time, and Continued to the Beginning of the Emperor Vespasian's Reign and the Total Destruction and Abolition of the Temple and Commonwealth of the Jews." by James Ussher 1650. From the Internet Sacred Text Archive, managed by John Bruno Hare.

10 Adam and Eve Tablet British Museum website 'Adam and Eve' cylinder seal Acquired from the John Robert Stewart Collection in 1846 T.C. Mitchell, The Bible in the British Museum (London, The British Museum Press,

1988) D. Collon, Catalogue of the Western Asi-1 (London, 1982) https://www.britishmuseum.org/explore/highlights/highlight_objects/me/a/adam_and_eve_cylinder_seal.aspx

11 Flavius Josephus.

12 *Romeo and Juliet,* William Shakespeare, Act 3, Scene 1.

13 *The Orthodox Jewish Bible.*

14 Flavius Josephus.

15 *The Orthodox Jewish Bible.*

16 *ISBE* (*International Standard Bible Encyclopedia*) From the International Standard Bible Encyclopedia Edited by James Orr, published in 1939 by Wm. B. Eerdmans Publishing Co. Website HTML © 2011. The specific text reference to Hebrews 10:33 is by Dr. A. Clarke on 1 Corinthians 4:9 and quotes Seneca, Ep. Vii. http://www.internationalstandardbible.com/G/gazing-stock.html "Gazing-stock"

17 Supernatural: Meetings with the Ancient Teachers of Mankind, Graham Hancock Disinformation Books; Revised edition (September 1, 2006)

18 The *Book of Enoch* I Translated by R.H. Charles, 1917. The Apocrypha and Pseudepigrapha of the Old Testament. Oxford: The Clarendon Press, 1913. (Fallen angels observed Earth and Heaven, 200 vowed to get human wives, Azâzêl is confined)

19 *The Orthodox Jewish Bible.*

20 *Jewish Encyclopedia*
http://www.jewishencyclopedia.com/
The unedited full-text of the 1906 Jewish Encyclopedia This website contains the complete contents of the 12-volume Jewish Encyclopedia, which was originally

published between 1901-1906. The Jewish Encyclopedia, which recently became part of the public domain, contains over 15,000 articles and illustrations.

This online version contains the unedited contents of the original encyclopedia. Since the original work was completed almost 100 years ago, it does not cover a significant portion of modern Jewish History (e.g., the creation of Israel, the Holocaust, etc.). However, it does contain an incredible amount of information that is remarkably relevant today. http://www.jewishencyclopedia.com/articles/13761-sin

Original Sin

Man is responsible for sin because he is endowed with free will ("behirah"); yet he is by nature frail, and the tendency of the mind is to evil: "For the imagination of man's heart is evil from his youth" (Gen. viii. 21; Yoma 20a; Sanh. 105a). Therefore God in His mercy allowed man to repent and be forgiven. Jewish theologians are divided in regard to the cause of this so-called "original sin"; some teach that it was due to Adam's yielding to temptation in eating of the forbidden fruit and has been inherited by his descendants; the majority, however, do not hold Adam responsible for the sins of mankind. The Zohar pictures Adam as receiving all the departed souls at his resting-place in the cave of Machpelah and inquiring of each soul the reason of its presence, whereupon the soul laments: "Woe unto me! thou art the cause of my departure from the world." Adam answers: "Verily, I have transgressed one precept and was punished; but see how many precepts and commandments of the Lord thou hast transgressed!" R. Jose said that every soul, before departing, visits Adam, and is convinced that it must blame its own wickedness, for there is no death without sin (Zohar, Bereshit, 57b). R. Hanina b. Dosa said: "It is not the wild ass that kills; it is sin that causes death" (Ber. 33a). On the other hand, it is maintained that at least four persons: Benjamin, Amram, Jesse, and Chileab; died without having committed any sin and merely as the result of Adam's weakness in yielding to the temptation of the serpent. To uphold the view of the majority, R. Ammi quoted the Scripture to show that sin causes pain and death: "I visit their transgression with the rod and their iniquity with stripes" (Ps. xxxix. 33); "The soul that sinneth, it shall die" (Ezek. xviii. 4). This verse is in contrast to another: "All things come alike to all: there is apparent one event to the righteous, and to the wicked" (Eccl. ix. 2; comp. Shab. 55a, b); but these two verses may perhaps be reconciled through others which declare "There is no man that sinneth not" (I Kings viii. 46); "For there is not a just man upon earth, that doeth good, and sinneth not" (Eccl. vii. 20; see Sanh. 105a).

21 Bluecloud Dakota Creation Legend Bluecloud Dakota Creation Legend from the Black Hills of Western South Dakota. "We Indians saw it as a beautiful place where we can go and pray and to receive something, perhaps, that is better than the gold that is in there. A lot of our creation stories and a lot of our Indian medicine came from the Black Hills.-Dog Eagle" http://www.webpanda.com/There/uot_lakota_sioux_creation_myth.htm

22 *The Orthodox Jewish Bible.*

23 *The Orthodox Jewish Bible.*

24 The *Book of Jubilees* from *"The Apocrypha and Pseudepigrapha of the Old Testament"* R.H. Charles Oxford: Clarendon Press, 1913

25 Flavius Josephus, *The Antiquities of the Jews,* 93 AD, Translator: William Whiston, *1737,* translator's note 8.

26 *Clark's Foreign Theological Library* Keil and Delitzsch (Multivolume Series) 1867ff Edinburgh T and T Clark, George Street Keil & Delitzsch Commentary on

the Old Testament Johann (C.F.) Keil (1807-1888) & Franz Delitzsch (1813-1890).

27 Ovid's *Metamorphoses,* Book 1,Translator John Dryden et al, 1717.

28 *Clark's Foreign Theological Library* Keil and Delitzsch.

29 The story of Ruatapu is a New Zealand legend from a tradition of the Ngati Porou, a Maori tribe of the east coast of New Zealand's North Island. *"Reedy, Anaru, Ngā Kōrero a Mohi Ruatapu, tohunga rongonui o Ngāti Porou": The Writings of Mohi Ruatapu* (Canterbury University Press: Christchurch, 1993), 142–146. http://teaohou.natlib.govt.nz/journals/teaohou/issue/Mao40TeA/c5.html

30 Raúl Erlando López in "The Antediluvian Patriarch and the Sumerian King List" First published in: *Journal of Creation* 12(3):347-357, 1998. Raúl E López has an M.S. and a Ph.D. in Atmospheric Science from Colorado State University. He worked for 23 years as a research meteorologist with the Environmental Research Laboratories of the National Oceanic and Atmospheric Administration. He has published about 50 journal papers and 90 conference papers and technical reports. Op Cit, quoting Walton, J., The antediluvian section of the Sumerian King List and Genesis 5, Biblical Archaeologist, 44:207-208, 1981. Also, see his later study on the Sumerian King List in *Ancient Israelite Literature in its Cultural Context*, Zondervan, pp. 127-31, 1989. http://creation.com/the-antediluvian-patriarchs-and-the-sumerian-king-list#txtRef2

31 *Epic of Atrahasis.*

32 Dr. David Livingston (PhD in Archeology Andrews University 1988)
Correlating the Texts of Ancient Literature with the Old

Testament © 2003 David Livingston
http://davelivingston.com/corancienttexts.htm

From the site "Ancient Days"

This site is to share with others the research done by Dr. David P. Livingston, Ph.D. We will keep posting new materials on archaeology, creation vs evolution, early man, ancient texts, the Flood, Exodus & Conquest.

The materials posted on this site are based on the belief that the Bible is God's Word and is relevant today. As Dr. Livingston encountered numerous attempts by historians, theologians, archaeologists and scientists to discount the validity of the Scriptures, he decided to try to meet these challenges. He began in 1967 by trying to resolve the archaeological problems encountered in the excavations at Jericho and Ai. To that end in 1969 he founded the Associates for Biblical Research (which he directed for 25 years), for the purpose of creating a think-tank for scholars and a resource for laymen.

Dr. Livingston has a Ph.D. in archaeology from Andrews University, an M.A. from Trinity graduate school in Deerfield, IL, an M.Div from Pittsburgh Theological Seminary, and a B.A from Wheaton College. He spent 10 years in Korea with his family from 1956 - 1966, including five years as the president of Kwan Dong College in KangNung, Korea. He initiated excavations at Khirbet Nisya (the"forgotten ruins"), in Israel, in 1979 as a result of his search for the Biblical city of Ai (and its neighbor, Bethel); he has directed excavations there for 24 years. He recently published his research in: Khirbet Nisya:
The Search for Biblical Ai 1979 - 2002

33 Yoruba Flood Legend The Yoruba people, one of the largest ethnic groups in Africa, live primarily in Nigeria. Some anthropologists believe these people had their origins in Canaan. Their ancestors may have been among

those driven out by the Israelite conquest of the land. [Hans Kelsen, in The Flood Myth, edited by Alan Dundes University of California Press Berkely and Los Angeles, California, University of California Press, Ltd., London, England, 1988 The Regents of the University of California.

34 Confucianism
S. Michael Houdmann, Question: "How to get to heaven - what are the ideas from the different religions?" Answer concerning Confucianism.,from the website *Got Question.org? The Bible has answers! We'll help you find them!*
http://www.gotquestions.org/how-to-get-to-heaven.html

35 Hinduism The blog post link below gives considerable detail about Hindu beliefs and practices and is especially interesting because it attempts to demonstrate parallels between Hinduism and Christianity, emphasizing the works-salvation aspects commonly understood by the world to be part of Christianity, as it truly is in most other faiths. This misconception about Christian belief is due largely to the influence of Roman Catholicism and other beliefs that add to the teachings of Scripture on salvation by grace through faith alone.
http://marbaniang.wordpress.com/2010/08/22/hinduism-4-stages-of-life-and-3-ways-of-salvation-parallels-with-christianity/

36 Buddhism Julia Hardy, "Afterlife and Salvation." Religion Library: Buddhism. *Patheos Library: Hosting the Conversation on Faith.* (No Date.)
http://www.patheos.com/Library/Buddhism/Beliefs/Afterlife-and-Salvation.html

Some Mahayana Buddhist monks aspired to become bodhisattvas, postponing the dissolution of self until all living things are enlightened. For seminal religious figures and heads of religious orders in Tibet, this took the unusual form of continued incarnations in human form as the same individual, lifetime after lifetime. The current Dalai Lama is called the 14th, for example, because this is believed to be his 14th incarnation as the Dalai Lama.

The notion of skillful means in Mahayana Buddhism led to other interpretations of salvation, such as rebirth in a Pure Land, where one could continue to aspire to enlightenment in pleasant surroundings without fear of rebirth in human form. Mahayana texts also refer to hells into which one might be reborn, usually in the context of rescuing others from a hellish domain, or transferring merit to those in such a place. There is also reference in the earliest texts to Yama, a deity of death who will judge and punish those who do evil. The punishment is not eternal, but lasts until the karma of these misdeeds has been exhausted.

As Buddhism evolved and as it moved to other countries with different religious backgrounds, other views of the afterlife emerged. Yama became a central figure in popular understandings of the afterlife in East Asia and also in Tibet. Tibetan Buddhists also envisioned the Bardo, a kind of limbo where the soul or self remained until the next rebirth.

In the Chinese tradition, where ancient notions of the role of the ancestors in human life have shaped Buddhism, people burned incense and paper goods depicting goods or money for the benefit of their deceased loved ones in order to provide a better situation for them in the afterlife. The deceased, in turn, were believed to be able to bring benefits or cause harm to the living.

Notions of heavens and hells eventually became a part of popular Buddhism throughout Asia. These range from ideal surroundings such as the Pure Lands to horrific worlds of punishment and suffering. Illustrated "hell texts" are popular among in some Buddhist countries, depicting in detail the punishments one can expect for a host of specific misdeeds, which may range from wearing tight blue jeans to murder.

As should be evident, there is no single, consistent notion of the afterlife and salvation within Buddhism. There are diverse and contradictory ideas even within individual countries. This is the result of the merging of Buddhism with pre-existing conceptions, of contradictions between scholarly and popular understandings, and of the evolution of ideas within Buddhism throughout the life of the religion.

37 Catholic Catechism, English translation of the Catechism of the Catholic Church for the United States of America copyright © 1994, United States Catholic Conference, Inc.: Libreria Editrice Vaticana. English translation of the Catechism of the Catholic Church: Modifications from the Editio Typica copyright © 1997, United States Catholic Conference, Inc.: Libreria Editrice Vaticana.

http://www.usccb.org/beliefs-and-teachings/what-we-believe/catechism/catechism-of-the-catholic-church/epub/index.cfm 400-401

38 Quran and Islam http://www.truthnet.org/islam/Quran/Rodwell/50/

Commentary on the Quran's view of Original Sin from The Origin and the Overcoming of Evil and Suffering in the World Religions edited by P. Koslowski Springer; 2002 edition (November 28, 2001).

"According to the Quran, both Adam and Eve together eat from the tree ... thus the Quran does not have Eve leading Adam astray nor her being the first to sin, and the concept of original sin that passes down through the generations to come is not emphasized. ... Given no

original sin, there is no need for atonement."
http://www.gotquestions.org/Islam.html

The Five Pillars of Islam

These five tenets compose the framework of obedience for Muslims:

1. The testimony of faith (shahada): "la ilaha illa allah. Muhammad rasul Allah." This means, "There is no deity but Allah. Muhammad is the messenger of Allah." A person can convert to Islam by stating this creed. The shahada shows that a Muslim believes in Allah alone as deity and believes that Muhammad reveals Allah.

2. Prayer (salat): Five ritual prayers must be performed every day.

3. Giving (zakat): This almsgiving is a certain percentage given once a year.

4. Fasting (sawm): Muslims fast during Ramadan in the ninth month of the Islamic calendar. They must not eat or drink from dawn until sunset.

5. Pilgrimage (hajj): If physically and financially possible, a Muslim must make the pilgrimage to Mecca in Saudi Arabia at least once. The hajj is performed in the twelfth month of the Islamic calendar.

A Muslim's entrance into paradise hinges on obedience to these Five Pillars. Still, Allah may reject them. Even Muhammad was not sure whether Allah would admit him to paradise (Surah 46:9; Hadith 5.266).
Read more:
http://www.gotquestions.org/Islam.html#ixzz2P8q6O6nI

39 *Clark's Foreign Theological Library* Keil and Delitzsch.
The genealogies in Gen 4 and 5, which trace the development of the human race through two fundamentally different lines, headed by Cain and Seth, are accompanied by a description of their moral development, and the statement that through marriages between the "sons of God" (Elohim) and the "daughters of men," the wickedness became so great, that God determined to destroy the men whom He had created. This description applies to the whole human race, and presupposes the intercourse or marriage of the Cainites with the Sethites.

Gen_6:1-2 relates to the increase of men generally (הָאָדָם, without any restriction), i.e., of the whole human race; and whilst the moral corruption is represented as universal, the whole human race, with the exception of Noah, who found grace before God (Gen_6:8), is described as ripe for destruction (Gen_6:3 and Gen_6:5-8). To understand this section, and appreciate the causes of this complete degeneracy of the race, we must first obtain a correct interpretation of the expressions "sons of God" (בני האלהים) and "daughters of men" (בנות האדם). Three different views have been entertained from the very earliest times: the "sons of God" being regarded as (a) the sons of princes, (b) angels, (c) the Sethites or godly men; and the "daughters of men," as the daughters (a) of people of the lower orders, (b) of mankind generally, (c) of the Cainites, or of the rest of mankind as contrasted with the godly or the children of God. Of these three views, the first, although it has become the traditional one in orthodox rabbinical Judaism, may be dismissed at once as not warranted by the usages of the language, and as altogether unscriptural. The second, on the contrary, may be defended on two plausible grounds: first, the fact that the "sons of God," in Job_1:6; Job_2:1, and Job_38:7, and in Dan_3:25, are unquestionably angels (also בְּנֵי אֵלִים in Psa_29:1 and Psa_89:7); and secondly, the antithesis, "sons of God" and "daughters of men." Apart from the context and tenor of the passage, these two points would lead us most naturally to regard the "sons of God" as angels, in distinction from men and the daughters of men. But this explanation, though the first to suggest itself, can only lay claim to be received as the correct one, provided the language itself admits of no other. Now that is not the case. For it is not to angels only that the term "sons of Elohim," or "sons of Elim," is applied; but in Psa_73:15, in an address to Elohim, the godly are called "the generation of Thy sons," i.e., sons of Elohim; in Deu_32:5 the Israelites are called His (God's) sons, and in Hos_1:10, "sons of the living God;" and in Psa_80:17, Israel is spoken of as the son, whom Elohim has made strong. These passages show that the expression "sons of God" cannot be elucidated by philological means, but must be interpreted by theology alone. Moreover, even when it is applied to the angels, it is questionable whether it is to be understood in a physical or ethical sense. The notion that "it is employed in a physical sense as nomen naturae, instead of angels as nomen officii, and presupposes generation of a physical kind," we must reject as an unscriptural and gnostic error. According to the scriptural view, the heavenly spirits are creatures of God, and not begotten from the divine essence. Moreover, all the other terms applied to the angels are ethical in their character. But if the title "sons of God" cannot involve the notion of physical generation, it cannot be restricted to celestial spirits, but is applicable to all beings which bear the image of God, or by virtue of their likeness to God participate in the glory, power, and blessedness of the divine life, - to men therefore as well as angels, since God has caused man to "want but little of Elohim," or to stand but a little behind Elohim (Psa_8:5), so that even magistrates are designated "Elohim, and sons of the

Most High" (Psa_82:6). When Delitzsch objects to the application of the expression "sons of Elohim" to pious men, because, "although the idea of a child of God may indeed have pointed, even in the O.T., beyond its theocratic limitation to Israel (Exo_4:22; Deu_14:1) towards a wider ethical signification (Psa_73:15; Pro_14:26), yet this extension and expansion were not so completed, that in historical prose the terms 'sons of God' (for which 'sons of Jehovah' should have been used to prevent mistake), and 'sons (or daughters) of men,' could be used to distinguish the children of God and the children of the world," - this argument rests upon the erroneous supposition, that the expression "sons of God" was introduced by Jehovah for the first time when He selected Israel to be the covenant nation. So much is true, indeed, that before the adoption of Israel as the first-born son of Jehovah (Exo_4:22), it would have been out of place to speak of sons of Jehovah; but the notion is false, or at least incapable of proof, that there were not children of God in the olden time, long before Abraham's call, and that, if there were, they could not have been called "sons of Elohim." The idea was not first introduced in connection with the theocracy, and extended thence to a more universal signification. It had its roots in the divine image, and therefore was general in its application from the very first; and it was not till God in the character of Jehovah chose Abraham and his seed to be the vehicles of salvation, and left the heathen nations to go their own way, that the expression received the specifically theocratic signification of "son of Jehovah," to be again liberated and expanded into the more comprehensive idea of υἱοθεσι´α τοῦ Θεοῦ (i.e., Elohim, not τοῦ κυρι´ου = Jehovah), at the coming of Christ, the Saviour of all nations. If in the olden time there were pious men who, like Enoch and Noah, walked with Elohim, or who, even if they did not stand in this close priestly relation to God, made the divine image a reality through their piety and fear of God, then there were sons (children) of God, for whom the only correct appellation was "sons of Elohim," since sonship to Jehovah was introduced with the call of Israel, so that it could only have been proleptically that the children of God in the old world could be called "sons of Jehovah." But if it be still argued, that in mere prose the term "sons of God" could not have been applied to children of God, or pious men, this would be equally applicable to "sons of Jehovah." On the other hand, there is this objection to our applying it to angels, that the pious, who walked with God and called upon the name of the Lord, had been mentioned just before, whereas no allusion had been made to angels, not even to their creation.

Again, the antithesis "sons of God" and "daughters of men" does not prove that the former were angels. It by no means follows, that because in Gen_6:1 האדם denotes man as a genus, i.e., the whole human race, it must do the same in Gen_6:2, where the expression "daughters of men" is determined by the antithesis "sons of God." And with reasons existing for understanding by the sons of God and the daughters of men two species of the genus האדם, mentioned in Gen_6:1, no valid objection can be offered to the restriction of האדם, through the antithesis Elohim, to all men with the exception of the sons of God; since this mode of expression is by no means unusual in Hebrew. "From the expression 'daughters of men," as Dettinger observes, "it by no means follows that the sons of God were not men; any more than it follows from Jer_32:20, where it is said that God had done miracles 'in Israel, and among men,' or from Isa_43:4, where God says He will give men for the Israelites, or from Jdg_16:7, where Samson says, that if he is bound with seven green withs he shall be as weak as a man, for from Psa_73:5, where it is said of the ungodly they are not in trouble as men, that the Israelites, or Samson, or the ungodly, were not men at all. In all these passages אדם (men) denotes the remainder of mankind in distinction from those who are especially named.” Cases occur, too, even in simple prose, in which the same term is used, first in a general, and then directly afterwards in a more restricted sense. We need cite only one, which occurs in Judges. In Jdg_19:30 reference is made to the coming of the children of Israel (i.e., of the twelve tribes) out of Egypt; and directly afterwards (Jdg_20:1-2) it is related that “all the children of Israel,” “all the tribes of Israel,” assembled together (to make war, as we learn from Jdg_20:3., upon Benjamin); and in the whole account of the war, Judges 20 and 21, the tribes of Israel are distinguished from the tribe of Benjamin: so that the expression “tribes of Israel” really means the rest of the tribes with the exception of Benjamin. And yet the Benjamites were Israelites. Why then should the fact that the sons of God are distinguished from the daughters of men prove that the former could not be men? There is not force enough in these two objections to compel us to adopt the conclusion that the sons of God were angels.

The question whether the “sons of Elohim” were celestial or terrestrial sons of God (angels or pious men of the family of Seth) can only be determined from the context, and from the substance of the passage itself, that is to say, from what is related respecting the conduct of the sons of God and its results. That the connection does not favour the idea of their being angels, is acknowledged even by those who adopt this view. “It cannot be denied,” says Delitzsch, “that the connection of Gen_6:1-8 with Gen 4 necessitates the assumption, that such intermarriages (of the Sethite and Cainite families) did take place about the time of the flood (cf. Mat_24:38; Luk_17:27); and the prohibition of mixed marriages under the law (Exo_34:16; cf. Gen_27:46; Gen_28:1.) also favours the same idea.” But this “assumption” is placed beyond all doubt, by what is here related of the sons of God. In Gen_6:2 it is stated that “the sons of God saw the daughters of men, that they were fair; and they took them wives of all which they chose,” i.e., of any with whose beauty they were charmed; and these wives bare children to them (Gen_6:4). Now לָקַח אִשָּׁה (to take a wife) is a standing expression throughout the whole of the Old Testament for the marriage relation established by God at the creation, and is never applied to πορνει´α, or the simple act of physical connection. This is quite sufficient of itself to exclude any reference to angels. For Christ Himself distinctly states that the angels cannot marry (Mat_22:30; Mar_12:25; cf. Luk_20:34.). And when Kurtz endeavours to weaken the force of these words of Christ, by arguing that they do not prove that it is impossible for angels so to fall from their original holiness as to sink into an unnatural state; this phrase has no meaning, unless by conclusive analogies, or the clear testimony of Scripture,

(Note: We cannot admit that there is any force in Hoffmann’s argument in his Schriftbeweis 1, p. 426, that “the begetting of children on the part of angels is not more irreconcilable with a nature that is not organized, like that of man, on the basis of sexual distinctions, than partaking of food is with a nature that is altogether spiritual; and yet food was eaten by the angels who visited Abraham.” For, in the first place, the eating in this case was a miracle wrought through the condescending grace of the omnipotent God, and furnishes no standard for judging what angels can do by their own power in rebellion against God. And in the second place, there is a considerable difference between the act of eating on the part of the angels of God who appeared in human shape, and the taking of wives and begetting of children on the part of sinning angels. We are quite unable also to accept as historical testimony, the myths of the heathen respecting demigods, sons of gods, and the begetting of children on the part of their gods, or the fables of the book of Enoch (ch. 6ff.) about the 200 angels, with their leaders, who lusted after the beautiful and delicate daughters of men, and who came down from heaven and took to themselves wives, with whom they begat giants of 3000 (or according to one MS 300) cubits in height.

Nor do 2Pe_2:4 and Jud_1:6 furnish any evidence of angel marriages. Peter is merely speaking of sinning angels in general (ἀγγε´λων ἁμαρτησα´ντων) whom God did not spare, and not of any particular sin on the part of a small number of angels; and Jude describes these angels as του`ς μη` τηρη´σαντας τη`ν ἑαυτῶν ἀρχη´ν ἀλλα` ἀπολιπο´ντας το` ἰ´διον οἰκητη´ριον, those who kept not their princedom, their position as rulers, but left their own habitation. There is nothing here about marriages with the daughters of men or the begetting of children, even if we refer the word του´τοις in the clause το`ν ὁ´μοιον του´τοις τρο´πον ἐκπορνευ´σασαι in Jud_1:7 to the angels mentioned in Jud_1:6; for ἐκπορνευ´ειν, the commission of fornication, would be altogether different from marriage, that is to say, from a conjugal bond that was permanent even though unnatural. But it is neither certain nor probable that this is the connection of του´τοις. Huther, the latest commentator upon this Epistle, who gives the preference to this explanation of του´τοις, and therefore cannot be accused of being biassed by doctrinal prejudices, says distinctly in the 2nd Ed. of his commentary, "του´τοις may be grammatically construed as referring to Sodom and Gomorrah, or per synesin to the inhabitants of these cities; but in that case the sin of Sodom and Gomorrah would only be mentioned indirectly." There is nothing in the rules of syntax, therefore, to prevent our connecting the word with Sodom and Gomorrah; and it is not a fact, that "grammaticae et logicae praecepta compel us to refer this word to the angels," as G. v. Zeschwitz says. But the very same reason which Huther assigns for not connecting it with Sodom and Gomorrah, may be also assigned for not connecting it with the angels, namely, that in that case the sin of the angels would only be mentioned indirectly. We regard Philippi's explanation (in his Glaubenslehre iii. p. 303) as a possible one, viz., that the word του´τοις refers back to the α´νθρωποι ἀσελγεῖς mentioned in Jud_1:4, and as by no means set aside by De Wette's objection, that the thought of Jud_1:8 would be anticipated in that case; for this objection is fully met by the circumstance, that not only does the word οὗτοι, which is repeated five times from Jud_1:8 onwards, refer back to these men, but even the word του´τοις in Jud_1:14 also. On the other hand, the reference of του´τοις to the angels is altogether precluded by the clause και` ἀπελθοῦσαι ὀπι´σω σαρκο`ς ἑτε´ρας, which follows the word ἐκπορνευ´σασαι. For fornication on the part of the angels could only consist in their going after flesh, or, as Hoffmann expresses it, "having to do with flesh, for which they were not created," but not in their going after other, or foreign flesh. There would be no sense in the word ἑτε´ρας unless those who were ἐκπορνευ´σαντες were themselves possessed of σα´ρξ; so that this is the only alternative, either we must attribute to the angels a σα´ρξ or fleshly body, or the idea of referring του´τοις to the angels must be given up. When Kurtz replies to this by saying that "to angels human bodies are quite as much a ἑτε´ρα σα´ρξ, i.e., a means of sensual gratification opposed to their nature and calling, as man can be to human man," he hides the difficulty, but does not remove it, by the ambiguous expression "opposed to their nature and calling." The ἑτε´ρα σα´ρξ must necessarily presuppose an ἰδι´α σα´ρξ.

But it is thought by some, that even if του´τοις in Jud_1:7 do not refer to the angels in Jud_1:6, the words of Jude agree so thoroughly with the tradition of the book of Enoch respecting the fall of the angels, that we must admit the allusion to the Enoch legend, and so indirectly to Gen 6, since Jude could not have expressed himself more clearly to persons who possessed the book of Enoch, or were acquainted with the tradition it contained. Now this conclusion would certainly be irresistible, if the only sin of the angels mentioned in the book of Enoch, as that for which they were kept in chains of darkness still the judgment-day, had been their intercourse with human wives. For the fact that Jude was acquainted with the legend of Enoch, and took for granted that the readers of his Epistle were so too, is evident from his introducing a prediction of Enoch in Jud_1:14, Jud_1:15, which is to be found in ch. i. 9 of Dillmann's edition of the book of Enoch. But it is admitted by all critical writers upon this book, that in the book of Enoch which has been edited by Dillmann, and is only to be found in an Ethiopic version, there are contradictory legends concerning the fall and judgment of the angels; that the book itself is composed of earlier and later materials; and that those very sections (ch. 6-16:106, etc.) in which the legend of the angel marriages is given without ambiguity, belong to the so-called book of Noah, i.e., to a later portion of the Enoch legend, which is opposed in many passages to the earlier legend. The fall of the angels is certainly often referred to in the earlier portions of the work; but among all the passages adduced by Dillmann in proof of this, there is only one (19:1) which mentions the angels who had taken wives. In the others, the only thing mentioned as the sin of the angels or of the hosts of Azazel, is the fact that they were subject to Satan, and seduced those who dwelt on the earth (54:3-6), or that they came down from heaven to earth, and revealed to the children of men what was hidden from them, and then led them astray to the commission of sin (64:2). There is nothing at all here about their taking wives. Moreover, in the earlier portions of the book, besides the fall of the angels, there is frequent reference made to a fall, i.e., an act of sin, on the part of the stars of heaven and the army of heaven, which transgressed the commandment of God before they rose, by not appearing at their appointed time (vid., 18:14-15; 21:3; 90:21, 24, etc.); and their punishment and place of punishment are described, in just the same manner as in the case of the wicked angels, as a prison, a lofty and horrible place in which the seven stars of heaven lie bound like great mountains and flaming with fire (21:2-3), as an abyss, narrow and deep, dreadful and dark, in which the star which fell first from heaven is lying, bound hand and foot (88:1, cf. 90:24). From these passages it is quite evident, that the legend concerning the fall of the angels and stars sprang out of Isa_24:21-22 ("And it shall come to pass in that day, that the Lord shall visit the host of the height [צְבָא הַמָּרוֹם, the host of heaven, by which stars and angels are to be understood on high i.e., the spiritual powers of the heavens] and the kings of the earth upon the earth, and they shall be gathered together, bound in the dungeon, and shut up in prison, and after many days they shall be punished"), along with Isa_14:12 ("How art thou fallen from heaven, thou beautiful morning star!"), and that the account of the sons of God in Gen 6, as interpreted by those who refer it to the angels, was afterwards combined and amalgamated with it.

Now if these different legends, describing the judgment upon the stars that fell from heaven, and the angels that followed Satan in seducing man, in just the same manner as the judgment upon the angels who begot giants from women, were in circulation at the time when the Epistle of Jude was written; we must not interpret the sin of the angels, referred to by Peter and Jude, in a one-sided manner, and arbitrarily connect it with only such passages of the book of Enoch as speak of angel marriages, to the entire disregard of all the other passages, which mention totally different sins as committed by the angels, that are punished with bands of darkness; but we must interpret it from what Jude himself has said concerning this sin, as Peter gives no further explanation of what he means by ἁμαρτῆσαι. Now the only sins that Jude mentions are μὴ τηρῆσαι τὴν ἑαυτῶν ἀρχήν and ἀπολιπεῖν τὸ ἴδιον οἰκητήριον. The two are closely connected. Through not keeping the ἀρχή (i.e., the position as rulers in heaven) which belonged to them, and was assigned them at their creation, the angels left “their own habitation” (ἴδιον οἰκητήριον); just as man, when he broke the commandment of God and failed to keep his position as ruler on earth, also lost “his own habitation” (ἴδιον οἰκητήριον), that is to say, not paradise alone, but the holy body of innocence also, so that he needed a covering for his nakedness, and will continue to need it, until we are “clothed upon with our hose which is from heaven” (οἰκητήριον ἡμῶν ἐξ οὐρανοῦ). In this description of the angels’ sin, there is not the slightest allusion to their leaving heaven to woo the beautiful daughters of men. The words may be very well interpreted, as they were by the earlier Christian theologians, as relating to the fall of Satan and his angels, to whom all that is said concerning their punishment fully applies. If Jude had had the πορνεία of the angels, mentioned in the Enoch legends, in his mind, he would have stated this distinctly, just as he does in v. 9 in the case of the legend concerning Michael and the devil, and in v. 11 in that of Enoch’s prophecy. There was all the more reason for his doing this, because not only to contradictory accounts of the sin of the angels occur in the Enoch legends, but a comparison of the parallels cited from the book of Enoch proves that he deviated from the Enoch legend in points of no little importance. Thus, for example, according to Enoch 54:3, “iron chains of immense weight” are prepared for the hosts of Azazel, to put them into the lowest hell, and cast them on that great day into the furnace with flaming fire. Now Jude and Peter say nothing about iron chains, and merely mention "everlasting chains under darkness" and "chains of darkness." Again, according to Enoch 10:12, the angel sinners are "bound fast under the earth for seventy generations, till the day of judgment and their completion, till the last judgment shall be held for all eternity." Peter and Jude make no allusion to this point of time, and the supporters of the angel marriages, therefore, have thought well to leave it out when quoting this parallel to Jud_1:6. Under these circumstances, the silence of the apostles as to either marriages or fornication on the part of the sinful angels, is a sure sign that they gave no credence to these fables of a Jewish gnosticizing tradition.)

it can be proved that the angels either possess by nature a material corporeality adequate to the contraction of a human marriage, or that by rebellion against their Creator they can acquire it, or that there are some creatures in heaven and on earth which, through sinful degeneracy, or by sinking into an unnatural state, can become possessed of the power, which they have not by nature, of generating and propagating their species. As man could indeed des/troy by sin the nature which he had received from his Creator, but could not by his own power restore it when destroyed, to say nothing of implanting an organ or a power that was wanting before; so we cannot believe that angels, through apostasy from God, could acquire sexual power of which they had previously been destitute.

Gen_6:3

The sentence of God upon the "sons of God" is also appropriate to men only. "Jehovah said: My spirit shall not rule in men for ever; in their wandering they are flesh." "The verb דּוּן = דִּין signifies to rule (hence אָדוֹן the ruler), and to judge, as the consequence of ruling. רוּחַ is the divine spirit of life bestowed upon man, the principle of physical and ethical, natural and spiritual life. This His spirit God will withdraw from man, and thereby put an end to their life and conduct. בְּשַׁגָּם is regarded by many as a particle, compounded of בְּ, שׁ a contraction of אֲשֶׁר, and גַּם (also), used in the sense of quoniam, because, (בְּשׁ = בַּאֲשֶׁר, as שׁ or שֶׁ = אֲשֶׁר Jdg_5:7; Jdg_6:17; Son_1:7). But the objection to this explanation is, that the גַּם, “because he also is flesh,” introduces an incongruous emphasis into the clause. We therefore prefer to regard שַׁגָּם as the inf. of שָׁגַג = שָׁגָה with the suffix: “in their erring (that of men) he (man as a genus) is flesh;” an explanation to which, to our mind, the extremely harsh change of number (they, he), is no objection, since many examples might be adduced of a similar change (vid., Hupfeld on Psa_5:10). Men, says God, have proved themselves by their erring and straying to be flesh, i.e., given up to the flesh, and incapable of being ruled by the Spirit of God and led back to the divine goal of their life. בָּשָׂר is used already in its ethical signification, like σα´ρξ in the New Testament, denoting not merely the natural corporeality of man, but his materiality as rendered ungodly by sin. “Therefore his days shall be 120 years:” this means, not that human life should in future never attain a greater age than 120 years, but that a respite of 120 years should still be granted to the human race. This sentence, as we may gather from the context, was made known to Noah in his 480th year, to be published by him as “preacher of righteousness” (2Pe_2:5) to the degenerate race. The reason why men had gone so far astray, that God determined to withdraw His spirit and give them up to destruction, was that the sons of God had taken wives of such of the daughters of men as they chose. Can this mean, because angels had formed marriages with the daughters of men? Even granting that such marriages, as being unnatural connections, would have led to the complete corruption of human nature; the men would in that case have been the tempted, and the real authors of the corruption would have been the angels. Why then should judgment fall upon the tempted alone? The judgments of God in the world are not executed with such partiality as this. And the supposition that nothing is said about the punishment of the angels, because the narrative has to do with the history of man, and the spiritual world is intentionally veiled as much as possible, does not meet the difficulty. If the sons of God were angels, the narrative is concerned not only with men, but with angels also; and it is not the custom of the Scriptures merely to relate the judgments which fall upon the tempted, and say nothing at all about the tempters. For the contrary, see Gen_3:14. If the "sons of God" were not men, so as to be included in the term אָדָם, the punishment would need to be specially pointed out in their case, and no deep revelations of the spiritual world would be required, since these celestial tempters would be living with men upon the earth, when they had taken wives from among their daughters. The judgments of God are not only free from all unrighteousness, but avoid every kind of partiality.

Gen_6:4

"The Nephilim were on the earth in those days, and also after that, when the sons of God came in unto the daughters of men, and they bare children to them: these are the heroes (הַגִּבֹּרִים) who from the olden time (מֵעוֹלָם, as in Psa_25:6; 1Sa_27:8) are the men of name" (i.e., noted, renowned or notorious men). נְפִילִים, from נָפַל to fall upon (Job_1:15; Jos_11:7), signifies the invaders (ἐπιπι΄πτοντες Aq., βιαΐοι Sym.). Luther gives the correct meaning, "tyrants:" they were called Nephilim because they fell upon the people and oppressed them.

(Note: The notion that the Nephilim were giants, to which the Sept. rendering γι΄γαντες has given rise, was rejected even by Luther as fabulous. He bases his view upon Jos_11:7 : “Nephilim non dictos a magnitudine corporum, sicut Rabbini putant, sed a tyrannide et oppressione quod vi grassati sint, nulla habita ratione legum aut honestatis, sed simpliciter indulgentes suis voluptatibus et cupiditatibus.” The opinion that giants are intended derives no support from Num_13:32-33. When the spies describe the land of Canaan as “a land that eateth up the inhabitants thereof,” and then add (Num_13:33), “and there we saw the Nephilim, the sons of Anak among (מִן lit., from, out of, in a partitive sense) the Nephilim,” by the side of whom they were as grasshoppers; the term Nephilim cannot signify giants, since the spies not only mention them especially along with the inhabitants of the land, who are described as people of great stature, but single out only a portion of the Nephilim as “sons of Anak” בְּנֵי עֲנָק), i.e., long-necked people or giants. The explanation “fallen from heaven” needs no refutation; inasmuch as the main element, “from heaven,” is a purely arbitrary addition.)

The meaning of the verse is a subject of dispute. To an unprejudiced mind, the words, as they stand, represent the Nephilim, who were on the earth in those days, as existing before the sons of God began to marry the daughters of men, and clearly distinguish them from the fruits of these marriages. הָיוּ can no more be rendered “they became, or arose,” in this connection, than הָיְתָה in Gen_1:2. וַיִּהְיוּ would have been the proper word. The expression “in those days” refers most naturally to the time when God pronounced the sentence upon the degenerate race; but it is so general and comprehensive a term, that it must not be confined exclusively to that time, not merely because the divine sentence was first pronounced after these marriages were contracted, and the marriages, if they did not produce the corruption, raised it to that fulness of iniquity which was ripe for the judgment, but still more because the words “after that” represent the marriages which drew down the judgment as an event that followed the appearance of the Nephilim. "The same were mighty men:" this might point back to the Nephilim; but it is a more natural supposition, that it refers to the children born to the sons of God. "These," i.e., the sons sprung from those marriages, "are the heroes, those renowned heroes of old."

Now if, according to the simple meaning of the passage, the Nephilim were in existence at the very time when the sons of God came in to the daughters of men, the appearance of the Nephilim cannot afford the slightest evidence that the "sons of God" were angels, by whom a family of monsters were begotten, whether demigods, daemons, or angel-men.

(Note: How thoroughly irreconcilable the contents of this verse are with the angel-hypothesis is evident from the strenuous efforts of its supporters to bring them into harmony with it. Thus, in Reuter's Repert., p. 7, Del. observes that the verse cannot be rendered in any but the following manner: "The giants were on the earth in those days, and also afterwards, when the sons of God went in to the daughters of men, these they bare to them, or rather, and these bare to them;" but, for all that, he gives this as the meaning of the words, "At the time of the divine determination to inflict punishment the giants arose, and also afterwards, when this unnatural connection between super-terrestrial and human beings continued, there arose such giants;" not only substituting "arose" for "were," but changing "when they connected themselves with them" into "when this connection continued." Nevertheless he is obliged to confess that "it is strange that this unnatural connection, which I also suppose to be the intermediate cause of the origin of the giants, should not be mentioned in the first clause of Gen_6:4." This is an admission that the text says nothing about the origin of the giants being traceable to the marriages of the sons of God, but that the commentators have been obliged to insert it in the text to save their angel marriages. Kurtz has tried three different explanations of this verse but they are all opposed to the rules of the language.) (1) In the History of the Old Covenant he gives this rendering: “Nephilim were on earth in these days, and that even after the sons of God had formed connections with the daughters of men;” in which he not only gives to גַּם the unsupportable meaning, “even, just,” but takes the imperfect יָבֹאוּ in the sense of the perfect בָּאוּ. (2) In his Ehen der Sφhne Gottes (p. 80) he gives the choice of this and the following rendering: “The Nephilim were on earth in those days, and also after this had happened, that the sons of God came to the daughters of men and begat children,” were the ungrammatical rendering of the imperfect as the perfect is artfully concealed by the interpolation of “after this had happened.” (3) In “die Sφhne Gottes,” p. 85: “In these days and also afterwards, when the sons of God came (continued to come) to the daughters of men, they bare to them (sc., Nephilim),” where יָבֹאוּ, they came, is arbitrarily altered into יוֹסִיפוּ לָבוֹא, they continued to come. But when he observes in defence of this quid pro quo, that “the imperfect denotes here, as Hengstenberg has correctly affirmed, and as so often is the case, an action frequently repeated in past times,” this remark only shows that he has neither understood the nature of the usage to which H. refers, nor what Ewald has said (§136) concerning the force and use of the imperfect.)

Gen_6:5-8

Now when the wickedness of man became great, and “every imagination of the thoughts of his heart was only evil the whole day,” i.e., continually and altogether evil, it repented God that He had made man, and He determined to destroy them. This determination and the motive assigned are also irreconcilable with the angel-theory. “Had the godless race, which God destroyed by the flood, sprung either entirely or in part from the marriage of angels to the daughters of men, it would no longer have been the race first created by God in Adam, but a grotesque product of the Adamitic factor created by God, and an entirely foreign and angelic factor” (Phil.).

(Note: When, on the other hand, the supporters of the angel marriages maintain that it is only on this interpretation that the necessity for the flood, i.e., for the complete destruction of the whole human race with the exception of righteous Noah, can be understood, not only is there no scriptural foundation for this argument, but it is decidedly at variance with those statements of the Scriptures, which speak of the corruption of the men whom God had created, and not of a race that had arisen through an unnatural connection of angels and men and forced their way into God’s creation. If it were really the case, that it would otherwise be impossible to understand where the necessity could lie, for all the rest of the human race to be destroyed and a new beginning to be made, whereas afterwards, when Abraham was chosen, the rest of the human race was not only spared, but preserved for subsequent participation in the blessings of salvation: we should only need to call Job to mind, who also could not comprehend the necessity for the fearful sufferings which overwhelmed him, and was unable to discover the justice of God, but who was afterwards taught a better lesson by God Himself, and reproved for his rash conclusions, as a sufficient proof of the deceptive and futile character of all such human reasoning.) But this is not the true state of the case. The Scriptures expressly affirm, that after the flood the moral corruption of man was the same as before the flood; for they describe it in Gen_8:21 in the very same words as in Gen_6:5 : and the reason they assign for the same judgment not being repeated, is simply the promise that

God would no more smite and destroy all living, as He had done before-an evident proof that God expected no change in human nature, and out of pure mercy and long-suffering would never send a second flood. "Now, if the race destroyed had been one that sprang from angel-fathers, it is difficult to understand why no improvement was to be looked for after the flood; for the repetition of any such unnatural angel-tragedy was certainly not probable, and still less inevitable" (Philippi).)

The force of יִנָּחֶם, "it repented the Lord," may be gathered from the explanatory יִתְעַצֵּב, "it grieved Him at His heart." This shows that the repentance of God does not presuppose any variableness in His nature of His purposes. In this sense God never repents of anything (1Sa_15:29), "quia nihil illi inopinatum vel non praevisum accidit" (Calvin). The repentance of God is an anthropomorphic expression for the pain of the divine love at the sin of man, and signifies that "God is hurt no less by the atrocious sins of men than if they pierced His heart with mortal anguish" (Calvin). The destruction of all, "from man unto beast," etc., is to be explained on the ground of the sovereignty of man upon the earth, the irrational creatures being created for him, and therefore involved in his fall. This destruction, however, was not to bring the human race to an end. "Noah found grace in the eyes of the Lord." In these words mercy is seen in the midst of wrath, pledging the preservation and restoration of humanity. (return to text)

(This concludes the section of Keil and Delitzsch)

40 Pastor Donald A. Adams, Pastor of Trinity Baptist Church, Weatherly PA. In the text of this work are emailed comments on the position that the Sons of God in Genesis 6 refers to descendants of Seth corrupting the godly line by intermarrying with female descendants of Cain. 11/18/2011

41 Flavius Josephus.

42 The *Book of Enoch*.

43 *The Chaldean Account of Genesis*.

44 The Epic of Shahnameh Ferdowsi http://www.enel.ucalgary.ca/People/far/hobbies/iran/shahnameh.html

(The Epic of Kings: Hero Tales of Ancient PersiaChapter 1The Shahs of Old (Zoroastrian). This is the translation of one of the world's greatest masterpieces The Epic of Shahnameh Ferdowsi (The Epic of Kings: Hero Tales of Ancient Persia) created by Hakim Abol-Ghasem Ferdowsi Toosi (940-1020) World famous Persian (Iranian) poet The Shahnameh or The Epic of Kings is one of the definite classics of the world. It tells hero tales of ancient Persia. The contents and the poet's style in describing the events takes the reader back to the ancient times and makes he/she sense and feel the events. Ferdowsi worked for thirty years to finish this masterpiece.

An important feature of this work is that during the period that Arabic language was known as the main language of science and literature, Ferdowsi used only Persian in his masterpiece. As Ferdowsi himself says "Persian language is revived by this work".

This is the translation of the *Epic of Shahnameh Ferdowsi* by Helen Zimmern.

45 The *Book of Jubilees*.

46 The Zadokite or Damascus Document was found both in the Cairo Geniza and at Qumran among the Dead Sea Scrolls. This text is not Scriptures, nor is it likely older than the Exile, but it speaks about conditions before the flood in a way that agrees with Scriptures. http://fam-faerch.dk/pseudigrapher/dsea/zadok01.html, (Webpage of Rolf Ivan Faerch)

47 Xochipilli

the Aztec god of art, games, beauty, dance, flowers, and song. His wife was believed to be a human girl named Mayahuel. He was among the gods responsible for fertility and agricultural produce. The Toltec civilization seems to have revered Xochipilli as a god favoring homosexuals and male prostitutes. Note the discussion later about his association with psychotropic substances. http://www.biroz.net/visions2012/xochipilli.htm

48 Kurupi and Pombero, http://www.ateneoguarani.edu.py/index.php?content=personajes_mitologicos

Kurupi is a god in Guarani mythology blamed for unexpected or unwanted pregnancies. (The Guaraní people live in south-central part of South America, especially in Paraguay and parts of the surrounding areas of Argentina, Brazil, and Bolivia.) The Pombero is a creature similar to descriptions of this god. Both were used to excuse adultery or explain ugly, excessively hairy or otherwise deformed children. They were also blamed for the disappearance of young women. Instead of taking responsibility for immorality, adultery, rape, or kidnapping, these people invented a "divine" being to excuse their sin. This invention might have even been used to justify abortion or exposure of unwanted or imperfect children.

49 Kamadeva/Madana http://www.sacred-texts.com/hin/hmvp/hmvp32.htm

(Hindu god) has a consort Rati, "whose very essence is desire". Sometimes he has two wives, Rati and Priti. He is spoken of as sneaking into Shiva's meditation chamber and, Cupid-like, shooting Shiva with an arrow intended to make him awaken and desire his wife. Shiva destroyed him for this invasion but resurrected him as a spirit being capable of spreading sexual desire throughout the world. He successfully tempted Shiva to give up meditation and unite with his wife to produce a child that would save the gods from an attack.

50 Freyr
Adam of Bremen, *Gesta Hammaburgensis Ecclesiae Pontificum,* Berlin, (translated and edited by G. Waitz, 1876).

This Norse God was associated with "sacral kingship" (being a priest, judge, and a ruler), virility and prosperity, with sunshine and fair weather, and was pictured as a fertility god. Freyr "bestows peace and pleasure on mortals". He is sometimes said to be an ancestor of the Swedish royal house.

51 *Cratylus* By Plato Written 360 B.C.E Translated by Benjamin Jowett
Plato Cratylus
http://classics.mit.edu/Plato/cratylus.html

52 Ovid's *Metamorphoses.* (Creation Story)
Before the seas, and this terrestrial ball, the World And Heav'n's high canopy, that covers all, One was the face of Nature; if a face: Rather a rude and indigested mass: A lifeless lump, unfashion'd, and unfram'd, Of jarring seeds; and justly Chaos nam'd. No sun was lighted up, the world to view; No moon did yet her blunted horns renew: Nor yet was Earth suspended in the sky, Nor pois'd, did on her own foundations lye: Nor seas about the shores their arms had thrown; But earth, and air, and water, were in one. Thus air was void of light, and earth unstable, And water's dark abyss unnavigable. No certain form on any was imprest; All were confus'd, and each disturb'd the rest. For hot and cold were in one body fixt; And soft with hard, and light with heavy mixt. But God, or Nature, while they thus contend, To these intestine discords put an end: Then earth from air, and seas from earth were driv'n, And grosser air sunk from aetherial Heav'n. Thus disembroil'd, they take their proper place;

The next of kin, contiguously embrace; And foes are sunder'd, by a larger space. The force of fire ascended first on high, And took its dwelling in the vaulted sky: Then air succeeds, in lightness next to fire; Whose atoms from unactive earth retire. Earth sinks beneath, and draws a num'rous throng Of pondrous, thick, unwieldy seeds along. About her coasts, unruly waters roar; And rising, on a ridge, insult the shore. Thus when the God, whatever God was he, Had form'd the whole, and made the parts agree, That no unequal portions might be found, He moulded Earth into a spacious round: Then with a breath, he gave the winds to blow; And bad the congregated waters flow. He adds the running springs, and standing lakes; And bounding banks for winding rivers makes. Some part, in Earth are swallow'd up, the most In ample oceans, disembogu'd, are lost. He shades the woods, the vallies he restrains With rocky mountains, and extends the plains. And as five zones th' aetherial regions bind, Five, correspondent, are to Earth assign'd: The sun with rays, directly darting down, Fires all beneath, and fries the middle zone: The two beneath the distant poles, complain Of endless winter, and perpetual rain. Betwixt th' extreams, two happier climates hold The temper that partakes of hot, and cold. The fields of liquid air, inclosing all, Surround the compass of this earthly ball: The lighter parts lye next the fires above; The grosser near the watry surface move: Thick clouds are spread, and storms engender there, And thunder's voice, which wretched mortals fear, And winds that on their wings cold winter bear. Nor were those blustring brethren left at large, On seas, and shores, their fury to discharge: Bound as they are, and circumscrib'd in place, They rend the world, resistless, where they pass; And mighty marks of mischief leave behind; Such is the rage of their tempestuous kind. First Eurus to the rising morn is sent (The regions of the balmy continent); And Eastern realms, where early Persians run, To greet the blest appearance of the sun. Westward, the wanton Zephyr wings his flight; Pleas'd with the remnants of departing light: Fierce Boreas, with his off-spring, issues forth T' invade the frozen waggon of the North. While frowning Auster seeks the Southern sphere; And rots, with endless rain, th' unwholsom year. High o'er the clouds, and empty realms of wind, The God a clearer space for Heav'n design'd; Where fields of light, and liquid aether flow; Purg'd from the pondrous dregs of Earth below. Scarce had the Pow'r distinguish'd these, when streight The stars, no longer overlaid with weight, Exert their heads, from underneath the mass; And upward shoot, and kindle as they pass, And with diffusive light adorn their heav'nly place. Then, every void of Nature to supply, With forms of Gods he fills the vacant sky: New herds of beasts he sends, the plains to share: New colonies of birds, to people air: And to their oozy beds, the finny fish repair. A creature of a more exalted kind Was wanting yet, and then was Man design'd: Conscious of thought, of more capacious breast, For empire form'd, and fit to rule the rest: Whether with particles of heav'nly fire The God of Nature did his soul inspire, Or Earth, but new divided from the sky, And, pliant, still retain'd th' aetherial energy: Which wise Prometheus temper'd into paste, And, mixt with living streams, the godlike image cast. Thus, while the mute creation downward bend Their sight, and to their earthly mother tend, Man looks aloft; and with erected eyes Beholds his own hereditary skies. From such rude principles our form began; And earth was metamorphos'd into Man.

53 The *Book of Enoch* I.

54 Antimony http://www.britannica.com/EBchecked/topic/28235/antimony-poisoning

55 Entheogen, Dictionary.com. Dictionary.com's 21st Century Lexicon. Dictionary.com http://dictionary.reference.com/browse/entheogen

56 A 16th-century Aztec statue of the god Xochipilli ("Prince of Flowers") was found near Tlalmanalco. Both the statue and the base are covered with carvings of psychoactive plants, including mushrooms, tobacco, and others. The figure has its head tilted upward. Its eyes are hollow-looking, the mouth half open, hands raised. It seems to be in a drug-induced state. The statue is in the Museo Nacional de Antropología in Mexico City.

57 The *Book of Enoch* I.

58 Ovid's *Metamorphoses*.

59 Catholic Catechism.

Bibliography

For links to most of the sources we used, as well as why and how we use certain references, and background and further information on sources, please consult the appendix.)

Adam of Bremen. *Gesta Hammaburgensis Ecclesiae Pontificum*. Berlin. (translated and edited by G. Waitz, 1876).

Adams, Donald A. Pastor of Trinity Baptist Church, Weatherly PA. In the text of this work are emailed comments on the position that the Sons of God in Genesis 6 refers to descendants of Seth corrupting the godly line by intermarrying with female descendants of Cain. 11/18/2011.

Anonymous. “Antimony Poisoning” article from *Encyclopaedia Britannica* online.

______. Artificial coal made from wood substance. *Journal of Chemical Education* (J. Chem. Educ.), January 1929.

______. Australian Aborigine “Dreaming” or “Dreamtime” Creation Story. Fulbright Foundation. The Australian American Educational Foundation, T/A the Australian American Fulbright Commission

______. “Big Five Mass Extinction Events.” Nature/Prehistoric Life. (No Date) *BBC.co.uk*

______. Bluecloud Dakota Creation Legend from the Black Hills of Western South Dakota. (No date.)

______. British Museum website. ‘Adam and Eve’ cylinder seal. Acquired from the John Robert Stewart Collection in 1846. T.C. Mitchell, *The Bible in the British Museum* (London, The British Museum Press, 1988) D. Collon, Catalogue of the Western Asi-1 (London, 1982). (References quoted in the description.)

______. “Burckle Crater: Dating the Flood.” (No date.) *Geocreationism.com*

______. Climate Change: “Melting Glaciers Expose Ancient Artifacts In Northern Europe Faster Than Archaeologists Can Collect Them.” *Huff Post Green* September 16, 2010. Video from Reuters, with Archaeologist Lars Piloe.

______. Climate Change Past and Future: The Ice Ages. “General Overview of the Ice Ages.” University of California, San Diego. Earthguide A part of the Geosciences Research Division at Scripps Institution of Oceanography.

______. “Comets and the Great Flood of Noah.” (No Date) *Creationism.org*

______. “CU-Boulder researchers hunt for artifact-rich glaciers.” INSTAAR (Institute of Arctic and Alpine Research) University of Colorado Boulder June 26 2002.

______. “‘Dinosaur Tree’ Behind Bars.” *Creation*. June 1, 2001. Answers in Genesis.

______. “Education: How are Gemesis lab-created diamonds made?” (No date.) Gemesis Website. http://gemesis.com (laboratory-produced diamonds)

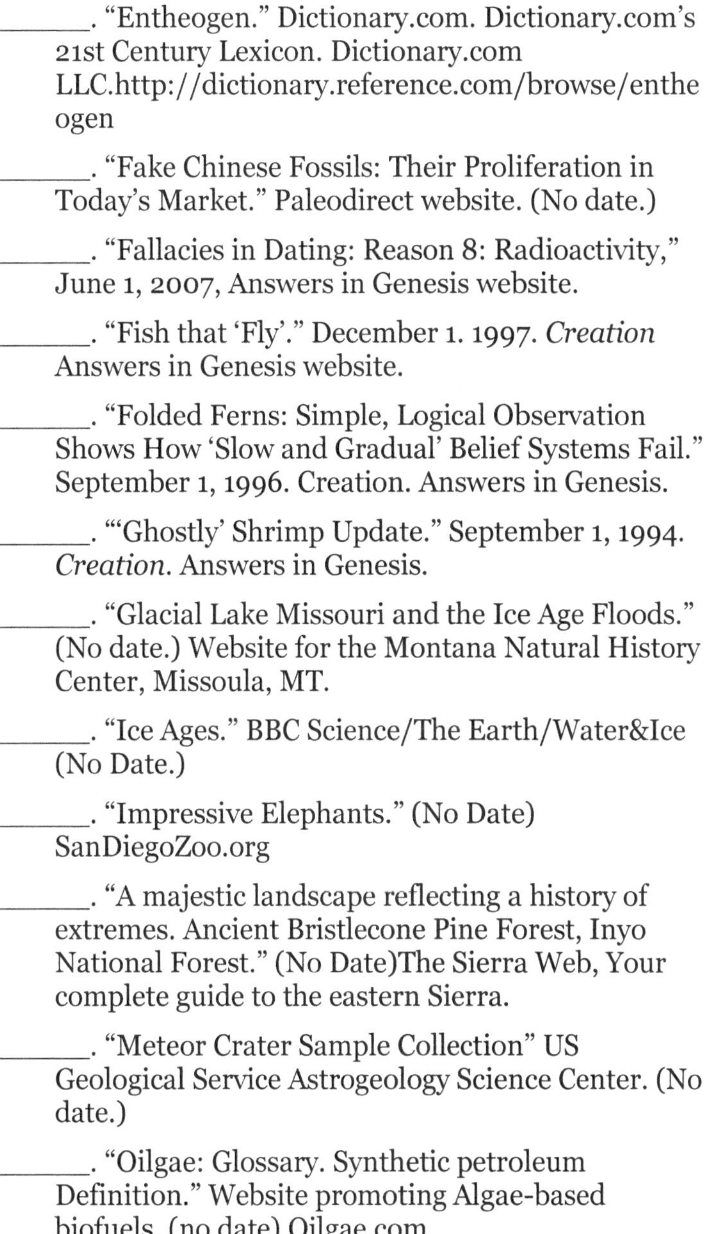

______. "Entheogen." Dictionary.com. Dictionary.com's 21st Century Lexicon. Dictionary.com LLC.http://dictionary.reference.com/browse/entheogen

______. "Fake Chinese Fossils: Their Proliferation in Today's Market." Paleodirect website. (No date.)

______. "Fallacies in Dating: Reason 8: Radioactivity," June 1, 2007, Answers in Genesis website.

______. "Fish that 'Fly'." December 1. 1997. *Creation* Answers in Genesis website.

______. "Folded Ferns: Simple, Logical Observation Shows How 'Slow and Gradual' Belief Systems Fail." September 1, 1996. Creation. Answers in Genesis.

______. "'Ghostly' Shrimp Update." September 1, 1994. *Creation*. Answers in Genesis.

______. "Glacial Lake Missouri and the Ice Age Floods." (No date.) Website for the Montana Natural History Center, Missoula, MT.

______. "Ice Ages." BBC Science/The Earth/Water&Ice (No Date.)

______. "Impressive Elephants." (No Date) SanDiegoZoo.org

______. "A majestic landscape reflecting a history of extremes. Ancient Bristlecone Pine Forest, Inyo National Forest." (No Date)The Sierra Web, Your complete guide to the eastern Sierra.

______. "Meteor Crater Sample Collection" US Geological Service Astrogeology Science Center. (No date.)

______. "Oilgae: Glossary. Synthetic petroleum Definition." Website promoting Algae-based biofuels. (no date) Oilgae.com

______. "Radiohalos." Wikipedia. Wikimedia Foundation Created by Jimmy Wales, Larry Sanger, Launched January 15, 2001.

______. "Rodent Resurrected." May 2, 2006. Answers in Genesis.

______. "Scientists Discover 356 Animal Inclusions Trapped In Opaque Amber 100 Million Years Old." European Synchrotron Radiation Facility. *ScienceDaily*. April 2008.

______. "Wonders of Geology: White Cliffs of Dover." August 21, 2008, Answers in Genesis.

Augustine. *City of God and Christian Doctrine,* Chapter 6, Book XI Translator, Schaff, Philip (1819-1893) Print Basis: New York: *The Christian Literature Publishing Co.*, 1890. (Electronic version from the Internet Sacred Text Archive, managed by John Bruno Hare.)

______ *Confessions* Book 11 Chapter XXX paragraph 41 . (Electronic version from the Internet Sacred Text Archive, managed by John Bruno Hare.)

Austin, S.A. *Ten misconceptions about the geologic column.* ICR *Impact,* No. 137, 1984.

Banks, Norm, photographer. "Pyroclastic Flow." 1980 photograph. U.S. Geological Survey

Barnosky, Anthony, et. al. "Has the Earth's sixth mass extinction already arrived?" *Nature* (International Weekly Journal of Science), 471, 51-57 (03 March 2011)

Barry, Sharon, et. al. "The Dynamic Earth: Geogallery." Smithsonian Website. (No Date)

Beatty, Kelly. "Chelyabinsk Mega-meteor: Status Report" June 25, 2013. Sky & Telescope The Essential Guide to Astronomy website.

Bellows, Henry Adams, translator. *The Poetic Edda* Princeton University Press and American Scandinavian Foundation, Princeton, NJ: 1936. From the Internet Sacred Text Archive, managed by John Bruno Hare.

Bosch, F. et al., "Observation of bound-state b: decay of fully ionized 187Re," Physical Review Letters 77(26)5190-5193, 1996. For further discussion of this experiment, see: Kienle, P., Beta-decay experiments and astrophysical implications, in: Prantzos, N. and Harissopulus, S., Proceedings, Nuclei in the Cosmos, pp. 181-186, 1999.

Brazo, Mark W. and Steven A. Austin. The Tunguska Explosion of 1908. Institute for Creation Research, Origins 9(2):82-93 (1982).

Brodeur, Arthur Gilchrist, translator. *The Prose Edda of Snorri Sturlson* New York: The American-Scandinavian Foundation, 1916. From the Internet Sacred Text Archive, managed by John Bruno Hare.

James Brooke. "Lost Worlds Rediscovered as Canadian Glaciers Melt." *New York Times on the Web Learning Network,* October 5, 1999.

Brown, Walt, Dr. "24. Missing Trunk." *In the Beginning: Compelling Evidence for Creation and the Flood.* Center for Scientific Creation 2008

Budge, E.A. Wallis, translator. *The Babylonian Legends of Creation.* 1921. "The Legend of the Creation According to Berosus and Damascius, written in Greek by Berosus, a priest of Bel-Marduk about 250 BC at Babylon from Alexander Polyhistor." from the

Internet Sacred Text Archive, managed by John Bruno Hare.

______. *The Book of the Cave of Treasures,* Part One (Brit. Mus. MS. Add. 25875.) [The Title of the Work: *The Scribe's Prayer* Translated from the Syriac by [London, The Religious Tract Society] [1927] {scanned and edited by Christopher M. Weimer, June 2002}
from the *Internet Sacred Text Archive* managed by John Bruno Hare.

______. A History of Creation. "The Book of knowing the Evolutions of Ra and of the overthrowing of Apep (Egyptian)". *Legends of the Gods, The Egyptian Texts.* London: Kegan Paul, Trench and Trübner & Co. Ltd., 1912. Scanned at sacred-texts.com 1999 and 2003. J.B. Hare, redactor.

Carney, Scott. "Did A Comet Cause The Great Flood?" *Discover Magazine,* November 15, 2007 re-posted in Free Republic Website.

Catchpoole, David. "Lea, the spaghetti lioness." *Creation* 29(4):44–45, September, 2007.

______. "The Lion that wouldn't eat meat." *Creation* 22(2):22–23 March, 2000.

Catholic Catechism, English translation of the Catechism of the Catholic Church for the United States of America copyright © 1994, United States Catholic Conference, Inc.—Libreria Editrice Vaticana. English translation of the Catechism of the Catholic Church: Modifications from the Editio Typica copyright © 1997, United States Catholic Conference, Inc.—Libreria Editrice Vaticana.

Charles, R. H., translator. The *Book of Enoch* I. *The Apocrypha and Pseudepigrapha of the Old Testament.* Oxford: The Clarendon Press, 1913.

From the Internet Sacred Text Archive, managed by John Bruno Hare.

_____. *Book of Jubilees,* The. The Society for Promoting Christian Knowledge, London, 1917. (Electronic version from the Internet Sacred Text Archive, managed by John Bruno Hare.)

_____. Zadokite or Damascus Document in *The Apocrypha and Pseudepigrapha of the Old Testament in English,* vol. 2: Pseudepigrapha (Oxford: Clarendon Press, 1913) http://fam-faerch.dk/pseudigrapher/dsea/zadok01.html, (Webpage of Rolf Ivan Faerch)

Cooper, David L, Dr. *Rules for Interpretation.* Biblical Research Monthly, 1947, 1949.

Cory, I. P. *Ancient Fragments* [1832 ed.] The Theology of the Phoenicians: From Sanchoniatho (reduced to HTML by Christopher M. Weimer, Dec. 2002) From the Internet Sacred Text Archive, managed by John Bruno Hare.

Dalley, Stephanie, translator. *Epic of Atrahasis -- Myths from Mesopotamia: Creation, the Flood, Gilgamesh, and Others* Oxford World's Classics. Oxford University Press, 1998.

Von Däniken, Erich. *Chariots of the Gods?* Penguin Group (USA) New York, NY January 1999.

Dawkins, Richard. *The Greatest Show on Earth: The Evidence for Evolution.* Free Press, Simon and Schuster, New York, NY, 2009.

Dimichele, William A. and Howard J. Falcoln-Lang. "Pennsylvania: 'fossil forests' in growth position (T° assemblages): origin, taphonomic bias and palaeoecological insights." Journal of the Geological Society, London, Vol. 168, 2011, pp. 585-605.

Dixon, Roland B. *Oceanic Mythology* Part I. "Polynesia Myths of Origins and the Deluge New Zealand," 1916(Electronic version from the Internet Sacred Text Archive, managed by John Bruno Hare.)

Doyle, Shaun, "Noah's comet? Was Noah's Flood a tsunami caused by a comet impact?" 2 January 2008. Creation.com

Edmonds, Molly. "How the Ice Age Worked" 13 May 2008. HowStuffWorks.com. http://geography.howstuffworks.com/terms-and-associations/ice-age.htm 12 April 2014.

Eldredge, Sandy and Bob Biek. "Ice Ages: What Are they and what causes them?" *Glad You Asked* article, Survey Notes, v. 42 no. 3, September 2010. Utah Geological Survey, Salt Lake City, UT.

Elias, Scott. Homepage. "Welcome to the World of Ice Age Paleoecology." University of Colorado at Boulder website.

Faulkner, Danny. "A biblically-based cratering theory." *Journal of Creation* 13(1):100-104 April 1999.

Felgenhauer, Joseph (Grand Canyon Park Ranger). "Inside Grand Canyon: How the Grand Canyon Was Shaped Over Time" (Transcript of oral presentation). National Park Service, U.S. Department of the Interior. Grand Canyon National Park, Arizona. (No Date.) National Park Service Website.

Ferdowsi, Hakim Abol-Ghasem (Toosi). *The Epic of Shahnameh Ferdowsi* (940-1020) Helen Zimmern translator. (*The Epic of Kings: Hero Tales of Ancient Persia* Chapter 1: The Shahs of Old (Zoroastrian). http://www.enel.ucalgary.ca/People/far/hobbies/iran/shahnameh.html

Findley, Michael J. *Rightly Dividing the Word of Truth. Elk Jerky for the Soul blog, August 6, 2012.*

Froede, Carl R. Jr. "Precambrian Plant Fossils and the Hakatai Shale Controversy." Volume 36(3):106-113 December 1999. Creation Research Society Quarterly Journal.

Gao, Ke-Qin & Neil H. Shubin. "Earliest known crown-group salamanders." *Nature* 422:428, March 27, 2003.

Gentry, Robert, Dr. "Creation's Tiny Mystery." Earth Science Associates 3rd edition (May 1992).

______ , et. al. "Fingerprints of Creation" video. Earth Science Associates Knoxville, TN, 1996.

Gish, Duane, Ph.D. "Origin of Life: Critique of Early Stage Chemical Evolution Theories." *Impact*. Institute for Creation Research, Jan 1, 1976

Goble, Phillip. *The Orthodox Jewish Bible*. English language version that applies Yiddish and Hasidic cultural expressions to the Messianic Bible. fourth edition. Copyright 2002,2003,2008,2010, 2011 by Artists for Israel International. All rights reserved.

Goetz, Delia and Sylvanus G. Morley, English translators. (Spanish translation by Adrián Recinos.) *Popol Vuh* ("Written Leaves") Book of the Mayas. The Book of the Community Book 1, copyright 1950 by the University of Oklahoma Press. (Electronic version from the Internet Sacred Text Archive, managed by John Bruno Hare.)

Gornitz, Vivien. "Sea Level Rise, After the Ice Melted and Today." *Science Briefs*. National Aeronautics and Space Administration Goddard Institute for Space Studies, January 2007.

Gould, Stephen Jay. "Nonoverlapping Magisteria," *Natural History* 106 (March 1997): 16-22. http://www.stephenjaygould.org/library/gould_noma.html

Halafta, Yose ben, rabi. *Seder Olam* or *Seder Olam Rabbah* (The Hebrew words mean "The Great Order of the World"). approximately 160 AD. English Translation of the *Seder Olam* http://www.betemunah.org/sederolam.html

Ham, Ken, Bodie Hodge, and Tim Chaffey. *Demolishing Supposed Bible Contradictions. Volumes 1, II. Master Books, Green Forest, AR, 2010.*

Hancock, Graham. *Fingerprints of the Gods*. Three Rivers Press. New York, NY, 1996.

_____. *Supernatural: Meetings with the Ancient Teachers of Mankind*. Disinformation Books. New York, NY, Revised edition 2006.

Hardy, Julia. "Afterlife and Salvation." Religion Library: Buddhism. *Patheos Library: Hosting the Conversation on Faith*. (No Date.)

Hawking, Stephen. *The Illustrated A Brief History of Time*. New York, NY: Bantam Dell, a division of Random House, 1996.

Heinlein, Robert A. *Time for the Stars*. Tor Books, New York, NY, 1956.

Herzenhorn, David M. "Lifted From a Russian Lake, a Big, if Fragile, Space Rock." October 16, 2013. New York Times website.

Hesiod. *The Theogony*. (ll. 116-138) Hugh G. Evelyn-White.translator. 1914. From the Internet Sacred Text Archive, managed by John Bruno Hare.

Hinduism http://marbaniang.wordpress.com/2010/08/22/hi

nduism-4-stages-of-life-and-3-ways-of-salvation-parallels-with-christianity/

Hitler, Adolph. *Mein Kampf.* Franz Eher Verlag (Publisher), Munich, Germany, 1925.

Hodge, Bodie. "Biblical Overview of the Flood Timeline." August 23, 2010 Answers in Genesis.

Hong, S.W. et al. Safety investigation of Noah's Ark in a seaway, *Journal of Creation* 8(1):26-36, 1994. (English version of a 1992 Korean study by on the seaworthiness of the ark supported by the Korea Association of Creation Research.) Proceedings of the International Conference on Creation Research, Korea Association of Creation Research, Taejon, 1993

Houdmann, S. Michael. Question: "How to get to heaven - what are the ideas from the different religions?" Answer concerning Confucianism. From the website *Got Question.org? The Bible has answers! We'll help you find them!*

Humphreys,D. Russell. *Earth's Magnetic Field is Decaying Steadily –with a Little Rhythm,* CRSQ (Creation Research Society Quarterly) July 1, 2010.

______. *Helium Diffusion Rates Support Accelerated Nuclear Decay* 2003 Abstract [in part] The entire paper is available for download as a .pdf file. http://logosresearchassociates.org/Documents/Baumgardner/Helium-Diffusion-Rates-Support-Accelerated-Nuclear-Decay.pdf

______. "Helium Evidence For A Young World Remains Crystal-Clear." Institute for Creation Research. April 27, 2005. The True Origin Archive.

______. "New time dilation helps creation cosmology." *Journal of Creation* 22(3):84–92 December 2008.

_____. *Starlight and Time: Solving the Puzzle of Distant Starlight in a Young Universe*. Master Books, Green Forest, AR, 1996.

Ilive, Thomas and M. M. Noah, translators (based on the Jewish Encyclopedia article). *Book of Jasher*, The. Also called *Sepher HaYasher*. Copyright Ken Johnson, 2013. Biblefacts Edition.
also; Salt Lake City, J.H. Parry and Company, 1887.

Inman, Mason. "New Asian Rodent Found as Food Is 'Living Fossil,' Gene Study Confirms." *National Geographic News*. April 24, 2007.

Jewish Encyclopedia
http://www.jewishencyclopedia.com/
The unedited full-text of the 1906 Jewish Encyclopedia

Josephus, Flavius. *Antiquities of the Jews , Book I.* William Whiston, translator. 1737. From the Internet Sacred Text Archive managed by John Bruno Hare.

Kelsen, Hans. *The Flood Myth*. Alan Dundes, editor. University of California Press: Berkely and Los Angeles, California, University of California Press, Ltd., London, England, The Regents of the University of California, 1988.

Al-Khatib, Talal. "Dino do-overs: Fixes to paleontology" Published August 14, 2013, *Discovery News*. *Foxnews.com/*Science

Kurtén, B. Pleistocene Mammals of Europe (Chicago: Aldine, 1968).

King, Leonard William. *The Seven Tablets of Creation.* Another Version of the Creation of the World by Marduk. Luzac's Semitic text and translation series. vol. xii-xiii Luzac and Co. London, 1902. From the

Internet Sacred Text Archive, managed by John Bruno Hare.

_____. *Enuma Elish* ("When on High") (Babylonian/Assyrian/Sumerian/ Chaldean/ Akkadian), Narration 1. London, 1902. From the Internet Sacred Text Archive, managed by John Bruno Hare.

Knapp, Alex. "Radioactive Decay Rates May Not Be Constant After All." *Forbes* Tech. May 3, 2011.

Larson, Kirsten. "Neutrinos!" IceCube South Pole Neutrino Observatory. National Science Foundation. University of Wisconson-Madison. (No date.)

Livingston, David, Jr., PhD. *Correlating the Texts of Ancient Literature with the Old Testament* © 2003 David Livingston http://davelivingston.com/corancienttexts.htm From the site "Ancient Days"

López, Raúl Erlando. "The Antediluvian Patriarch and the Sumerian King List." *Journal of Creation* 12(3):347-357, 1998.

McDonald, Charlotte. "Who, What, Why: Is the Earth getting lighter?" BBC News Magazine, 31 January, 2012.

McDowell, Josh. *New Evidence That Demands a Verdict*. Thomas Nelson; Nashville, TN. 1st edition, 1999.

Meyer, T. and J. Martin. *Clark's Foreign Theological Library* 1854-1858. Keil and Delitszch (Multivolume Series) 1867ff Edinburgh T and T Clark, George Street Keil & Delitzsch Commentary on the Old Testament Johann (C.F.) Keil (1807-1888) & Franz Delitzsch (1813-1890).

Miller, Brandon. "Presto! Instant Petrified Wood Created in Lab." Tech. January 27, 2005. LiveScience website.

Morris, J. 2010. "The Real Nature of the Fossil Record." *Acts & Facts*. 39 (2): 12-14. Institute for Creation Research.

Mortenson, Terry, Dr. "Fossil Turtles Confound Evolutionists." April 18, 2005. Answers in Genesis.

Munro IR, Guyuron B "Split-Rib Cranioplasty". *Annals of Plastic Surgery* 7 (5): 341-346, November 1981.

Murray, Richard. "Missouri Watershed Profile." 14 November 2013. Prezi.com (A site for creating and sharing presentations.)

Naso, Publius Ovidius. (Ovid) The *Metamorphoses,* Book 1. John Dryden, et al, translators, 1717. From the Internet Sacred Text Archive, managed by John Bruno Hare.

Oard, Michael J. "Chapter 8: The Snowblitz, October 1, 2004." From the book *Frozen in Time,* Masterbooks, a division of New Leaf Press (Green Forest, Arkansas) 2004.

______. "The Geological Column Is a General Flood Order with Many Exceptions." *The Geologic Column: Perspectives Within Diluvial Geology*. Reed, J.K and M.J. Oard (editors). Creation Research Society.

______. "How did 90% of large Australian Ice Age animals go extinct?" *Journal of Creation* 22(1):17–19, April 2008.

______. *The New Answers Book Where Does The Ice Age Fit?* Master Books, Green Forest, AR, 2007.

O'Neil, Dennis, Dr. "Interpreting the Fossil Record." RECORD OF TIME: An Introduction to the Nature of Fossils and Paleoanthropological Dating Methods. Website created and maintained by , Behavioral Sciences Department, Palomar College, San Marcos, California Copyright © 1998-2012 by Dennis O'Neil. All rights reserved.

Orr, James, editor. *ISBE* (*International Standard Bible Encyclopedia*) originally published in 1939 by Wm. B. Eerdmans Publishing Co. Website HTML copyright 2011.

Parker, Gary. Dr. "Fossil Plants." *Creation Facts of Life, Answers in Genesis website,* January 1, 1994.

______. "How Fast?" *Creation Facts of Life, Answers in Genesis website,* January 1, 1994.

Plato. *Cratylus*. 360 B.C.E Benjamin Jowett, translator.

Post, Vincent, Dr. et al. News and Media Media release: "Scientists find vast new freshwater sources under the sea." 05 Dec 2013 The National Centre for Groundwater Research and Training is an Australian Government initiative, supported by the Australian Research Council and the National Water Commission.

______ "Offshore fresh groundwater reserves as global phenomenon." *Nature* 504, 71-78 (05 Dec 2013). International weekly journal of science. Nature.com

Quran and Islam http://www.truthnet.org/islam/Quran/Rodwell/50/

Reedy, Anaru, *Ngā Kōrero a Mohi Ruatapu, tohunga rongonui o Ngāti Porou: The Writings of Mohi Ruatapu.* Canterbury University Press: Christchurch, 1993.

Remy, Melina. ("Our Amazing Planet" staff writer.) "The World's Longest Rivers." June 23, 2010. Livescience.com

Riddle, Mike, "Does Radiometric Dating Prove the Earth Is Old?" October 4, 2007 Excerpted from *The New Answers Book,* Answers in Genesis. Master Books/New Leaf Press: Green Forest, AR, 2006.

Roys, Ralph L. *The Book of Chilam Balam of Chumayel* (Mayan), XIII ("The Creation of the Uinal")Washington, D.C.:Carnagie Institution, 1933. From the Internet Sacred Text Archive, managed by John Bruno Hare.

Ruse, M. "Leading anti-creationist philosopher admits that evolution is a religion. How Evolution Became a Religion: Creationists Correct?" *National Post*, pp. B1, B3, B7 May 13, 2000.

Russell, Eric. "The Biology Classics: Paramecium Reproduction." Biomedia Associates: Learning Programs for Biology Education. (No Date.) Beaufort, SC.

Sachs, Mendel, Dr. from his website.

St. John, James. "Replacement." (Fossil preservation involving change in crystal structure and mineralogy of an organism's hard parts.) (No date) Ohio State University at Newark Website.

Sarfati, Jonathan. "Flood models and biblical realism." Journal of Creation 24(3):46–53 December 2010.

______. "How did dinosaurs grow so big?" Creation 28(1):44–47 December 2005

______. *'Millions of years' are missing*. (Interview with biologist and geologist Ariel Roth.) Creation.com

Sawyer, Diane. "Stephen Hawking on Religion: 'Science Will Win,'" Interview with Diane Sawyer, as quoted on ABC World News (07 June 2010).

Scheven, Joachim. "Living Fossils." Creation. September 1, 1993. Answers in Genesis.

Shakespeare, William. *Romeo and Juliet.* Act 3, Scene 1.

Sherwin, F. 2006. Amber: A Window to the Recent Past. *Acts & Facts*. 35 (7). Institute for Creation Research.

Shoemaker, Eugene M. "Impact Mechanics at Meteor Crater, Arizona." Prepared on behalf of the U.S. Atomic Energy Commission. US Geological service Publications.

Smith, George. *The Chaldean Account of Genesis*. London: Thomas Scott, 1876. From the Internet Sacred Text Archive, managed by John Bruno Hare.

Snelling, Andrew A., PhD. The Cause of Anomalous Potassium-Argon "Ages" for Recent Andesite Flows at Mt. Ngauruhoe, New Zealand, and the Implications for Potassium-Argon "Dating" Answers in Genesis Presented at the Fourth International Conference on Creationism, Pittsburgh, Pennsylvania, August 3–8, 1998. Published in: Proceedings of the Fourth International Conference on Creationism, R. E. Walsh (editor), pp. 503–525.

_____. "Coal Beds and Noah's Flood." June 1, 1986. Creation Ex Nihilo; Answers in Genesis.

_____. "Did Meteors Trigger Noah's Flood?" December 6, 2011, Answers in Genesis website.

_____. "The Earth's magnetic field and the age of the Earth," first published: *Creation (Creation Ministries International)*, 13(4):44-48 September 1991.

______. "The Fallacies of Radioactive Dating of Rocks: Basalt Lava Flows in Grand Canyon. *Answers*. Sept. 5, 2006.

______. "Order in the Fossil Record." November 23, 2009. *Answers*. Answers in Genesis.

______. "Polonium Radiohalos: Still 'A Very Tiny Mystery'." *Acts & Facts*. 29 (8). 2000.

______. Radioactive "Dating" Failure: Recent New Zealand Lava Flows Yield "Ages" of Millions of Years. December 1, 1999. Creation Answers in Genesis website.

______. "Radiocarbons in Diamonds Confirmed." November 7, 2007. AiG-U.S. (Answers in Genesis website).

______. Radiohalos: The Flood's Smoking Gun. (Three-Part series) Answers in Genesis Website.
1. Mysterious Bullet Holes in Rocks March 5, 2012
2. Radiohalos: The Mysterious Vanishing Bullets June 6, 2012
3. Solving the Mystery of the Missing Bullets. Sept. 11, 2012

______. "Radioisotope Dating of Rocks in the Grand Canyon." June 1, 2005. Creation Answers in Genesis website.

______. "Snelling's Reply to Gentry." Nov 17, 2002. Earth Science Associates website.

______. "The World's a Graveyard: Flood Evidence Number Two." Answers in Genesis. February 12, 2008

Solomon, S., et. al., (eds.). "Changes Before the Industrial Era?" IPCC, 2007: Climate Change 2007: The Physical Science Basis. Contribution of Working Group I to the Fourth Assessment Report of the

Intergovernmental Panel on Climate Change. Cambridge University Press, Cambridge, United Kingdom and New York, NY, USA.

Spence, Lewis. *The Myths of Mexico and Peru,* 1913. Garcia's *Origin de los Indias* (Translation of Mixtec picture-manuscript) quoted in this work.

Swanson, D.A., (photographer). Phreatic Eruption, Mount St. Helens 18 May 1980.

Swenson, Keith. "Radio-Dating in Rubble: The Lava Dome at Mount St Helens Debunks Dating Methods." Creation Magazine June 1, 2001 Answers in Genesis Website.

al-Tabari, Ibn Jarir. (Muslim historian 838-923.) *The History of al-Tabari.* English translation of *The History of the Prophets and Kings.*

Than, Ker. "Huge Ocean Discovered Inside Earth." February 28, 2007. Livescience.comTharpar, Romila. *Frontline* magazine Volume 18, Issue 19, Sep. 15-28, 2001.

Theoi Classical E-Texts Library, New Zealand.

Thom, Harrie. "How could Noah care for the animals?" Creation 30(1):50–51, December 2007.

Thomas, Brian, M.S. "Canadian 'Mega' Dinosaur Bonebed Formed by Watery Catastrophe." July 13, 2010. Institute for Creation Research.

______. "Chinese Dinosaurs Were Fossilized by Flood." April 8. 2011. Institute for Creation Research.

______. Dinosaur Fossil "Wasn't Supposed to Be There." April 14, 2011. Institute for Creation Research. icr.org

Ussher, James. The Annals of the World "The Origin of Time, and Continued to the Beginning of the

Emperor Vespasian's Reign and the Total Destruction and Abolition of the Temple and Commonwealth of the Jews." London: Printed by E. Tyler for F. Crook and B. Bedell, 1658. From the Internet Sacred Text Archive, managed by John Bruno Hare.

U.S. Geological Survey. Geologic Names Committee, 2010, Divisions of geologic time—major chronostratigraphic and geochronologic units: U.S. Geological Survey Fact Sheet 2010–3059, 2 p.

______. Graphic of Index Fossils. http://pubs.usgs.gov/gip/geotime/fossils.html

Valentine, J. W. "How Good Was the Fossil Record? Clues from the California Pleistocene," *Paleobiology* 15 no. 2 (1989): 83 -94.

Vardiman, Larry, Ph.D. Scientific Naturalism as Science. *Acts & Facts* (Institute for Creation Research), 26 (11). 1997.

______. and D. R. Humphreys. 2010. *A New Creationist Cosmology: In No Time at All* Part 1. Acts & Facts. 39 (11): 12-15, 40 (1): 12-14, 40(2): 12-14.

Velikovsky, Immanuel. *Ages in Chaos.* Harper, New York, NY, 1950.

______. *Worlds in Collison.* Harper, New York, NY, 1950.

Voth. H.R. Hurúing Wuhti and the Sun. From Field Columbian Museum Publication 96 Anthropological Series Volume VIII, The Traditions of the Hopi. The Stanley McCormick Hopi Expedition George A Dorsey, Curator, Department of Anthropology, Chicago, IL March, 1905 Scanned, proofed and formatted at sacred-texts.com, February 2001, by John Bruno Hare. Reformatted, August 2003. From the Internet Sacred Text Archive, managed by John Bruno Hare.

Walker, Tas. Walker/Klevberg chart. "Time/Rock Transformation" Chart based on the Walker system modifed by Klevberg. Tas Walker's Biblical Geology website.

WELLINGTON. *"THE SAMOAN STORY OF CREATION-A 'Tala.' " JOURNAL OF THE POLYNESIAN SOCIETY CONTAINING THE TRANSACTIONS AND PROCEEDINGS OF THE SOCIETY. VOL. I.* [Wellington, 1892] {Reduced to HTML by Christopher M. Weimer, November 2002

West, E.W., translator. Narration 28 Bundahis, Chapter I, "In the name of the creator Aûharmazd." (Persian) *Sacred Books of the East,* Volume 5, Oxford: the Clarendon Press, 1880. From the Internet Sacred Text Archive, managed by John Bruno Hare.

_____. *Pahlavi Texts.* Part V "Marvels of Zoroastrianism." *Sacred Books of the East,* Volume 47 Oxford: the Clarendon Press, 1897. From the Internet Sacred Text Archive, managed by John Bruno Hare.

Whitten, D.G.A. and J.R.V. Brooks. The Penguin Dictionary of Geology. Middlesex, England: Penguin Books, 1972.

Wilkins, W. J. *Hindu Mythology, Vedic and Puranic.* Calcutta: Thacker, Spink & Co.; London: W. Thacker & Co. 1900. Kamadeva/Madana. From the Internet Sacred Text Archive, managed by John Bruno Hare.

Wise, K. "The Fossil Record: The Ultimate Test Case for Young-Earth Creationism," Opus: A Journal for Interdisciplinary Studies (1991-92): 17-29. Answers in Genesis.

Woodmorappe, John. "Billion-Fold Acceleration of Radioactivity Demonstrated in Laboratory." Journal of Creation. Answers in Genesis. August 1, 2001.

_____. "Caring for the Animals on the Ark." March 29, 2007. *Answers*. Answers in Genesis. (This may be a valuable source, given that the author's *Feasibility Study* book is out of print. See entry below.)

_____. "*National Geographic* Plays the Dating Game." April 1, 2002. Answers in Genesis website.

_____. *Noah's Ark: A Feasibility Study*. Institute for Creation Research, Dallas, TX, July 1996.

Woody, Todd. "Gulf oil spill methane bloom disappears." *Grist: A Beacon in the Smog*. January 7, 2011.

Woolley, Joanna F. "The Origin of the Carboniferous Coal Measures Part 1: Lessons from History" Journal of Creation 24(3):76–81.

Xocipilli information: http://www.biroz.net/visions2012/xochipilli.htm

Zenkova, Olga. "Libra did not survive the severity of Chelyabinsk meteorite." (Translation provided on the site page. It is in Russian). Novosti website, 10/16/2013.

How Much Is Enough?

How Much Is Enough? Miscellaneous Appendixes

A. Uniformitarian Answer Appendix

This material contains uniformitarian responses and beliefs in greater detail than can be contained in the main text. It is included to be fair and honest.

Mclean v Arkansas Board of Education

The following is testimony of Dr. G. Brent Dalrymple under oath in December 1981 representing the ACLU. The text of the trial transcript is from *Creation's Tiny Mystery* by Dr. Robert V Gentry, p. 122 and following.

Q I think you stated earlier that you reviewed quite a bit of creation-science literature in preparation for your testimony in this case and also a case in California, is that correct?

A Yes. I think I've read either in whole or in part about two dozen books and articles.

Q But on the list of books that you made or articles that you have reviewed, you did not include any of Robert Gentry's work as having been reviewed, did you?

A That's right. I did not.

Q Although you consider Gentry to be a creation scientist?

A Well, yes. But, you know, the scientific literature and even the Creation Science literature, which I do not consider scientific literature. It's outside the traditional literature: there is an enormously complex business. There is a lot of it. And we can't review it all. Every time I review even a short paper, it takes me several hours to read it, I have to think about the logic involved in the data, I have to reread it several times to be sure I understand what the author has said; I have to go back through the author's references and sometimes read [p. 122] as many as twenty or thirty papers that the author has referenced to find out whether what has been referenced is true or makes any sense; I have to check the calculations to find out if they are correct. It's an enormous job. And given the limited amount of time that I have to put in on this, reviewing the Creation Science literature is not a terribly productive thing for a scientist to do.

Q How many articles or books have you reviewed, approximately?

A You mean in Creation Science literature?

Q Creation Science literature.

A I think it was approximately twenty-four or twenty-five, something like that, as best I can remember. I gave you a complete list, which is as accurate as I can recall.

Q And if there were articles in the open scientific literature: Excuse me; in refereed journals which supported the Creation Science model, would that not be something you would want to look at in trying to review the Creation Science literature? A Yes, and I did look at a number of those. And I still found no evidence.

Q But you didn't look at any from Mr. Gentry?

A No, I did not. That's one I didn't get around to. There's quite a few others I haven't gotten around to. I probably never will look into all the creationists' literature. I can't even look into all the legitimate scientific literature. But I can go so far as to say that every case that I have looked into in detail has had very, very serious flaws. And I think I've looked at a representative sample.

And also in Gentry's work, he's proposed *a very tiny mystery* which is balanced on the other side by an enormous amount of evidence. And I think it's important to know what the answer to that little mystery is. But I don't think you can take one little fact for which we now have no answer, and try to balance, say that equals a preponderance of evidence on the other side. That's just not quite the way the scales tip.

Answer (Continuing) Okay, sir. The experiment that Doctor Gentry proposed ...

THE COURT: Let me ask you a question. As I understand it, that's his conclusion. I still don't understand what his theory is.

THE WITNESS: [Dalrymple]: He [Gentry] has proposed that it is either a theory or a hypothesis that he says can be falsified.

THE COURT: What's the basis for the proposal? How does he come up with that?

THE WITNESS: Well, basically what he has found is there is a series of radioactive haloes within minerals in the rocks. Many minerals like mica include very tiny particles of other minerals that are radioactive, little crystals of zircon and things like that, that have a lot of uranium in them.

And as the uranium decays, the alpha particles will not decay, but travel outward through the mica. And they cause radiation damage in the mica around the radioactive particle. And the distance that those particles travel is indicated by these radioactive haloes. And that distance is related directly to the energy of the decay. And from the energy of the decay, it is thought that we can identify the isotopes.

That's the kind of work that Gentry has been doing.

And what he has found is that he has identified certain haloes which he claims are from Pollonium-212 [sic, polonium-218; correct form of the chemical elements used hereafter]. Now, polonium-218 is one of the isotopes intermediate in the decay chain between uranium and lead.

Uranium doesn't decay directly from [sic, to] lead. It goes through a whole series of intermediate products, each of which is radioactive and in turn decays.

Polonium-218 is derived in this occasion from radon-222. And what he has found is that the polonium haloes, and this is what he claims to have found, are the polonium-218 haloes, but not radon-222 haloes. And therefore, he says that the polonium could not have come from the decay of radium, therefore it could not have come from the normal decay change [sic, chains].

And he says, how did it get there? And then he says that the only way it could have gotten there unsupported by radon-222 decay is to have been primordial polonium, that is polonium that was created at the time the solar system was created, or the universe.

Well, the problem with that is polonium-218 has a half-life of only about three minutes, I believe it is. So that if you have a granitic body, a rock that comes

> from the melt, that contains this mica, and it cools down, it takes millions of years for a body like that to cool.
>
> [p. 126]
>
> So that by the time the body cooled, all the polonium would have decayed, since it has an extremely short half-life. Therefore, there would be no polonium in the body to cause the polonium haloes.
>
> So what he is saying, this is primordial polonium; therefore, the granite mass in which it occurs could not have cooled slowly; therefore, it must have been created by fiat, instantly.
>
> And the experiment he has proposed to falsify this is that he says he will accept this hypothesis as false when somebody can synthesize a piece of granite in the laboratory.
>
> And I'm claiming that that would be a meaningless experiment.
>
> Does that ... know this is a rather complicated subject.
>
> THE COURT: I am not sure I understand all of this process. Obviously I don't understand all of this process, but why don't you go ahead, Mr. Ennis?

Wikipedia is more straightforward, but takes the same position using the same reasoning. In a 2013 article they say, "The most widely accepted explanation is that the discolouration is caused by alpha particles emitted by the nuclei; the radius of the concentric shells are proportional to the particle's energy (Henderson & Bateson 1934) The phenomenon of radiohalos has been known to geologists since the early part of the 20th century, but wider interest was prompted by the claims of creationist Robert V. Gentry that radiohalos in biotite are evidence for a young earth (Gentry 1992). These claims are rejected by the scientific community as an example of creationist pseudoscience (Wakefield 1988)."

http://en.wikipedia.org/wiki/Radiohalo

The sentences are juxtapositioned to say that Creationists do not believe the Henderson & Bateson paper. That is not true.

The Geology of Gentry's "Tiny Mystery." 1988 by J.R. Wakefield is the source cited by Wikipedia as "proof" of "creationist pseudoscience." The opening abstract says, "The unusual polonium halos described by Robert Gentry have been a problem for some years now. Gentry claimed that the polonium halos show that the Precambrian granite they are hosted in were 'instantly created.'

Some research on the halos has been carried out by other scientists, but most of it has been aimed at solving the problems of the peculiar configuration of these halos. Fortunately, Gentry provided two specific site locations in the Canadian Shield where his samples came from. The geological setting of these sites shows conclusively that Gentry's notion of an 'instantly created' earth composed of granite is false. Specifically the samples came from crystallized rocks which can be shown to crosscut several sedimentary and other plutonic rocks. Some of the sedimentary rocks contain stromatolites. The geology of the sites shows that the uranium, and most likely the polonium, were deposited via postmagmatic hydrothermal fluids. Besides ignoring the geology at his collection areas, Gentry also makes numerous grossly erroneous generalizations about the origin of plutonic rocks."

His introduction includes "The polonium halos constitute a case of misinterpretation because Gentry's preconceived ideas blinded him to some very important facts. His work has been devoted solely to the physics of the halos, and he has completely neglected the geological setting of the samples in which the halos are found. The result is the same though, a false conclusion reached because of an unjustified expectation of what the data should show.

"In both cases conclusions vindicating preconceived religious convictions were desired so badly that often scientific integrity was compromised, intentionally or inadvertently" (Hastings. 1982, p. 51-52)

Because of his apparent ignorance of geology, Gentry makes numerous unwarranted generalizations about the nature of the world's Precambrian rocks. The purpose of this paper is to explain the geological setting of three of Gentry's sample sites. The geology at each of these sites clearly shows that the samples came from uranium-rich dikes that crosscut many other pre-existing rocks, including sedimentary rocks. Thus, Gentry's claims are disproven and provide a clear example of a creationist researcher (Gentry) misinterpreting his data."

The first page of the body of his paper, after three pages of attacks on creationists, finally states his thesis. "I do not intend to discuss the physics of halos in this paper. What I will describe here is the geology of three of the locations where some of Gentry's biotite samples came from - the Fission Mine, the Silver Crater Mine and the Faraday Mine, all near Bancroft in southern Ontario (see Figure 1). On the basis of the geology of the sample sites. I will hypothesize that the uranium, and hence the polonium, were deposited by precipitation from circulating fluids."

All of J.R. Wakefield boils down to 1) He is not going to "discuss the physics of halos" and 2) "the uranium, and hence the polonium, were deposited by precipitation from circulating fluids."

The rest of this paper is immaterial because his second point is exactly the position of the majority of creationists. The mechanism of *how* that happened, which determines *when* it happened is the issue, but that is not discussed in this paper. So nothing in the cited source supports *Wikipedia's* false assertion that Creationism is Pseudoscience.

TalkOrigins is a website devoted to promoting uniformitarianism and evolution, but aimed at creationists. It is designed to sound "unbiased" and "impartial." It is frequently a good reference to cite when dealing with uniformitarians because they will accept the information on this site more readily. They frequently obfuscate, so if you go to their site, read very, very carefully.
http://www.talkorigins.org/faqs/po-halos/gentry.html
"Igneous rocks form from molten material, and are further subdivided into two main categories, the volcanic rocks which form from lava extruded at or near the surface; and plutonic rocks which form from magma, deep within the crust."
"Plutonic rocks on the other hand cool very slowly, on the order of a million years or more for some deeply buried and insulated magmas."
[This information is near the top of the first page. Notice that "million of years" is a dogmatic assertion. Remember the earlier warnings to look for their assumptions. Their assertions are based on their assumptions.]
"Granite is a well-known type of plutonic igneous rock..."
[Building on the assertion that plutonic rock is millions of years old, their meaning here is that granite is therefore "well-known" to be millions of years old.]

"Radiation damage haloes around mineral inclusions are well known from the geological literature. Discoloration haloes in younger rocks tend to be smaller and less

intense than in older rocks, indicating that the zone of crystal damage increases with time. From these observations early attempts were made to use the dimensions of haloes as an age dating technique. This was never fully successful as the size/intensity of an observed damage halo was also a function of the abundance of radionuclides present in the inclusion, and the crystalline structure of the host mineral."
[The most important point is in the last sentence. "Age dating" [is]"never fully successful as...observed damage halo was also a function of...the crystalline structure of the host mineral." This is the same argument used earlier. The "crystalline structure of the host mineral" is assumed to be millions of years old, therefore the radiohalos are millions of years old because they are found in the "crystalline structure of the host mineral." Please note the very devious form of circular reasoning.]

"Gentry's thesis has several components. [?] First is his contention that the granitic rocks from which samples reportedly came constitute the 'primordial' crust of the Earth. Within these rocks are biotite (an iron-bearing form of mica) and fluorite crystals which bear a relatively uncommon class of tiny, concentric discoloration 'haloes'." [Biotite and fluorite crystals in granite containing radiohaloes is an observable fact. The phrase "from which samples reportedly came" is a slanderous attack on the reliability of the scientist performing the test. This is especially egregious since the tests have been repeated multiple times by several organizations with identical results.]

"Gentry utilized microscope thin sections of rocks from samples sent to him by others from various places around the world. [Very true] Thus, he is unable to say how his samples fit in with the local or regional geological setting(s). He also does not provide descriptive information about the individual rock samples that make up his studies - i.e., the abundance and distribution of major, accessory, or trace minerals; the texture, crystal size and alteration features of the rocks; and the presence or absence of fractures and discontinuities." [This statement places a burden of proof on *TalkOrigins* to prove how and why any of the listed variables would alter Dr. Gentry's published results.]

"Gentry does not acknowledge that the Precambrian time period represents fully 7/8 of the history of the Earth [another very true statement, but still not fulfilling their requirement of burden of proof] as determined by decades of intensive field and laboratory investigations by thousands of geologists. [This is their "proof." For centuries, it was necessary to believe in bloodletting to become an M.D. Just simply being in the majority and working hard does not mean that you are correct.] Consequently, he does not recognize the wide diversity of geologic terranes that came and went over that enormous time span." [The only two pieces of "evidence" presented by Talkorigins in this article that there ever was an "enormous time span" are 1) we say so and 2) "thousands of geologists" did 'intensive field and laboratory investigations." If you believe that this misrepresents Talkorigins, we provided a direct link to this article which you may read for yourself and draw your own conclusions.]

Dr. Gentry's "claim that his samples represent 'primordial' basement rocks is patently incorrect." [Even if you believe this statement to be correct, this is not science. It is just a gratuitous assertion. Like *Wikipedia, Talkorigins* cites the flawed Wakefield report as evidence.]

"In Gentry's model..." "Gentry provides no explanation..." "Gentry's hypothesis would seem to suggest..." [This is classic straw man logical fallacy. A scientific theory begun in 1918 and modified by many scientists for nearly a century is assigned to just one person and they then proceed to assassinate his character. This classic form of character assassination is what creationists are falsely accused of. By this point in the Talkorigins article they invent the term "polonium halo hypothesis." Since radiohalos forms by the decay of polonium, leaving radiohalos, and this is an observed and proven concept, this is not a hypothesis.]

"... It is apparent that the association of concentric colored haloes with polonium is actually speculative." [This is just one more unsupported, gratuitous assertion. Probably the most serious error of this entire article is ignoring the work other creationists have done in this field for the past thirty years. There are many answers in many creationist journals to every single problem they raise. *ICR (the Institute for Creation Research),* and *AIG (Answers In Genesis), Creation Ministries International* are the most well-known, but there are many others. The article spends much time and effort pointing out that water transport is the most likely cause of polonium radiohalos. It seems odd that they are completely unaware that this is the creationist position. It is also the reason creation scientists have concluded that the evidence is in favor of a flood time period for the formation of radiohalos.]

B. Flood Legends Appendix

In this appendix we hope to point out and explain some things that are often not included in studies about the flood legends of other cultures. Some people are not aware that so many flood legends exist in cultures all over the world. Some don't realize how ancient some of these legends are.

It is important to point out that although there may be as many as 500 flood legends from around the world, many of them bear little similarity to the biblical narrative and likely only represent local floods or other isolated incidents. We have said before that many mythologies were created by rulers to consolidate their power in self-worship. Those would have made an effort to bury or discredit any truth of the Scriptures.

But there are cultures where some truth has remained buried in men's memories. The "common source" many anthropologists talk about is likely the post-flood preservation efforts and ministry of Noah and his descendants. This attempt to teach truth was disrupted by the building of the tower at Babel. That sin was judged by the confusion of languages at Babel. Small amounts of truth still followed man everywhere at the dividing and dispersing of people throughout the earth.

Anthropologists dismiss many of these similarities as "cultural corruption" by missionaries, but the missionaries themselves expressed amazement that these people already knew parts of what they were trying to teach them from the Bible. The knowledge was flawed and error-filled, but some of it was evidence of God's miraculous preservation of His truth through the ages.

TalkOrigins has a large, comprehensive list of these legends. http://www.talkorigins.org/faqs/flood-myths.html

The main purpose of this site, however, is to point out inconsistencies and discrepancies in the biblical account, to discredit scriptural truth, so its information must be taken with careful scrutiny. It does have many accounts which can be studied, compared with other sources, and analyzed for whatever value they have.

Variations of the chart included here appear on many creationist sites. It tries to list key elements of the Genesis account of the flood, along with 20+ representative flood legends of cultures around the world, and to show where these accounts have similarities and differences. Most sites that reproduce a chart similar to this one give as a source the following work:

B.C. Nelson, *The Deluge Story in Stone,* Appendix 11, Flood Traditions, Figure 38, Augsburg, Minneapolis, 1931.

It also has a later edition:

The Deluge Story in Stone, B. C. Nelson, 1968, 2nd ed., Bethany Fellowship, Minneapolis, Minnesota, pp. 165-176.

Our chart is adapted from several sources, including

http://nwcreation.net/noahlegends.html

http://www.answersingenesis.org/articles/am/v2/n2/flood-legends and http://www.earthage.org/floodlegends/flood__legends.htm

It is not a perfect chart, a perfect list of points of comparison, or, by any means, an exhaustive list of flood legends. We include it as an example of how these similarities can be studied more easily.

For each specific point in the Genesis account, the chart shows whether a flood legend from another culture includes the item ("Flood due to man's sin", for example, occurs in eight of the charted legends), does not include it (eleven of the accounts do not say that God vowed complete destruction), or has a partial similarity to the Scripture (six have some degree of similarity to the statement that Noah was to build a vessel).

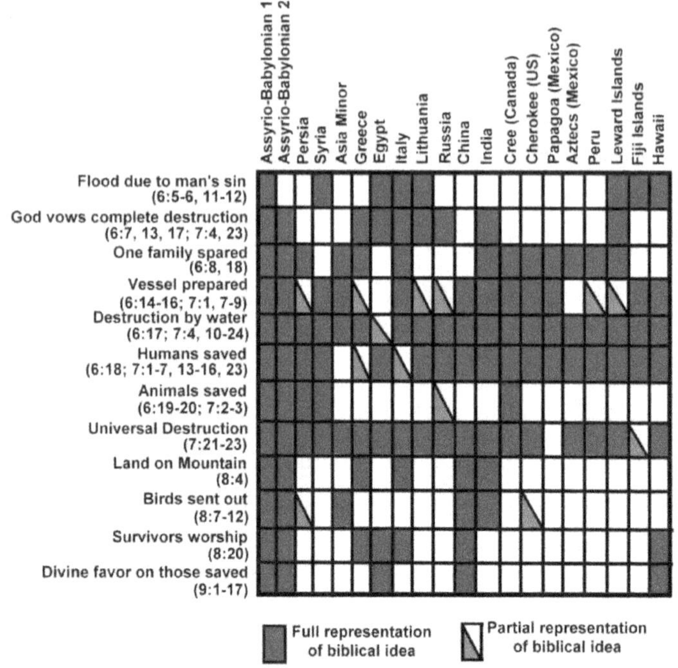

"Full representation of biblical idea" means that the creator of the chart believed the flood legend contains a close approximation of the scriptural account, not that it was exactly the same. Examples of these close approximations show up in the Assyrian/Babylonian/ Akkadian/Sumerian legends. Many elements seem to be very similar to the scriptural truth, but it is not really correct to say all the items in the chart are "full representations".

For example, some variants of the Mesopotamian legends state that the gods were merely annoyed with human noise or that there were simply too many people, instead of being clear on the flood's purpose of destroying the evil men and their works. Some state that one god had to go behind the others' backs to warn his favorite, rather than saying that the man was righteous as opposed to the other people's evil.

The Persian (also middle-eastern roughly where modern-day Iran is located) legends describe it as a battle between good and evil and make no mention of saving any humans, merely of destroying and disposing of the evildoers. The Zoroastrian Persian flood legend includes this passage, however:

"[Ahura Mazda, the Creator, told] Yima [the earthly ruler] to build a vara, a large square enclosure, in which to keep specimens of small and large cattle, human beings, dogs, birds, red flaming fires, plants and foodstuffs, two of every kind. The men and cattle he brought in were to be the finest on earth."

It is similar to the biblical account but describes a shelter rather than a floating vessel.

When speaking about a particular culture's flood legend, it is wise to remember that it may not be one simple version. The *Epic of Gilgamesh* is one of the oldest and most well-known ancient written documents, yet multiple versions of the story exist in thousands of fragments of clay tablets throughout the ancient archaeological sites of the middle east. It includes a flood legend that has many similarities to the biblical account.

An Aboriginal (Australian) Flood Legend is the subject of a Creation Magazine article by Howard Coates from October 1, 1981.

"This is an old time story told by the earliest, profoundly knowledgeable elders," said Mickie Bungunie [an old man from the Wunambal Aborigine tribe, Western Australia].

http://www.answersingenesis.org/articles/cm/v4/n3/aboriginal-flood-legend

This statement by the Aborigine tribe's representative is similar to the message of many of these native people. Their response to the question about whether the story is "real" or simply something they were told by white men is that it is ancient. The *Epic of Gilgamesh* is considered older than the seventh century B.C.

Legends of a flood in China's texts are found as early as 1000 B.C., in the *Book of Odes* and in the *Book of Documents*. The *Book of Documents* has some of the earliest writings of the Chinese, even older than bone oracle inscriptions of China. This book contains a flood story that runs as follows: "The flood waters were everywhere, destroying everything as they rose above the hills and swelled up to Heaven."

A Chinese flood story with the exact detail that eight people were saved is found in a document called the Huai-nan-tzu, dated from the 2nd century B.C.

The *Red Record* or "Wallam Olum" includes a flood story and is a pictographic record made by the Lenni Lenape (Delaware) Indians of their ancient history. In 1820 a doctor in Indiana tended a sick Lenni Lenape record keeper and received this pictoral history from him.

An account from the Masai tribe in Africa has so many similarities to the biblical flood record it is often dismissed as contamination but the people insist it is their own record, older than their contact with white men.

A Spanish historian, Herrera, recorded flood stories of the Incas in Peru. He said, "The ancient Indians reported, they had received it by tradition from their ancestors, [and that the flood took place] many years before the Incas ... "

http://www.ecreationscience.com/Flood_Legends.html

The Cowichan people of the Salish, Native Americans of Montana and the Northwest Coast insist that their flood legend comes from a time "long before the missionaries ever arrived ... " This account also says that many wise men had the same dream of rain or floods and came together to build a great raft, which scoffers ignored and ridiculed. This parallels ancient Jewish traditional accounts recorded by Josephus, stating that Adam, Enoch, and Methuselah all had warnings about the flood, though theirs were less clear and specific than Noah's.

The Salish legend also says that after the survivors of the flood began to resettle and multiply, the began to quarrel again as they had before, and ended up dividing into separate tribes and moving away.

http://www.firstpeople.us/FP-Html-Legends/TheGreatFlood-Salish.html

A large number of flood legends have the survivors climb a high mountain rather than get in a ship. Some commentators say that may be a result of confusion with the beginning and ending of the biblical flood account, but another explanation seems more likely. We have talked in this volume about the probability that Noah built the ark on the highest point of land in existence at that time, and the reasons why that may have been the case. If these scattered people recalled that fact but lost the truth about the ark, perhaps they recounted the idea that going to the highest ground meant safety because that was all they remembered.

This topic is something we will cover again when we study World Literature in module 5 of this series. The legends are a part of the literature of these people, even if they are oral traditions.

While we do not endorse everything taught by the following sites, we include the list below as reference.

They are some links that can be used for further study of the flood legends:

From the *Institute for Creation Research*

A fairly short article for this organization, non-technical, that does a good job of distilling the importance of this topic.

http://www.icr.org/article/why-does-nearly-every-culture-have-tradition-globa/

From Creation.com

A simple list with little commentary and some quotes from the original sources, and a bibliography of sources covering this topic.

http://creation.com/many-flood-legends

From Talkorigins.org

(Remember that this is a secular site, but it is a very well-researched and comprehensive list)

http://www.talkorigins.org/faqs/flood-myths.html

From *Apologetics Press*

Brief discussion of major legends and their importance, and a bibliography

http://www.apologeticspress.org/apcontent.aspx?category=9&article=64

From Northwest Creation Network

Includes different charts of legends compared with the biblical account, plus a number of legend summaries, and many links to other related articles.

http://www.nwcreation.net/noahlegends.html

From *Conservapedia*

http://www.conservapedia.com/Great_Flood

Answers in Genesis

Good, brief summary of the importance of studying this topic and a few comparative stories

http://www.answersingenesis.org/articles/am/v2/n2/flood-legends

Jewish History

This is a really great perspective on scriptural authority and personal choice. Well worth a read -through for a modern cultural perspective, but caution is advised when it comes to the account of Noah's "post-traumatic stress syndrome". The admonition that "there is something to be afraid of" is a little obscure, making it sound as if they believe there could be another worldwide cataclysm, but taking it to mean that we have an all-powerful God Who punishes sin is good.

http://www.jewishhistory.org/the-great-flood/

Cumorah.com

This is a Latter Day Saints site but has large, clear images and handwritten copies of ancient cuneiform tablets, with somewhat technical, critical analysis of flood legend studies.

http://www.cumorah.com/index.php?target=view_other_articles&story_id=59&cat_id=7

The best gift you can give an author

is an honest, thoughtful review. Please consider leaving one online. Help us understand what you liked and didn't like about the book and why. Help authors reach more readers and spread your influence and ours. If you liked the book, please recommend it to your spouse, friends, pastors, teachers, cashiers, employers, – anybody and everybody you see each day. If you don't know what to say, remember Proverb 16:3 – Commit thy works unto the Lord and thy thoughts shall be established. Thank you!

OTHER BOOKS AND PRODUCTS FROM FINDLEY FAMILY VIDEO PUBLICATIONS

All our books (including Historical Fiction, SciFi, contemporary relationships short stories, and an Archaeological Mystery serial) are linked on our blog.

Elk Jerky for the Soul includes posts on current issues, excerpts from our fiction and nonfiction works, Bible teaching, travel and everyday observations, and more.

http://findleyfamilyvideopublications.com/

Visit our YouTube Channel

https://www.youtube.com/channel/UCGhwNpU115ARMwgYwTIJBrA/featured. Book trailers, video excerpts, project teasers, and more. Science, History, Literature, and biblical worldview studies are the focus of our book and video projects.

Historical Fiction

by Michael J. Findley

The Ephron the Hittite Series (Including boxed set of all titles)

Ephron Son of Zohar

Tawananna Daughter of Zohar

Heth Son of Canaan Son of Ham, Noah

Shelometh Daughter of Yovov Wife of Ephron

Zita Son of Ephron and Shelometh

Adult Romantic Suspense

by Mary C. Findley

The Men of the Realmlands series

Book One: The Baron's Ring

Book Two: The Captain's Blade

Send a White Rose

Chasing the Texas Wind

Carrie's Hired Hand (novella)

Young Adult Historical Adventure

by Mary C. Findley

Hope and the Knight of the Black Lion (plus illustrated version)

The Benny and the Bank Robber Series

Benny and the Bank Robber (Plus homeschool editions for student and teacher with review and vocabulary)

Doctor Dad

The Oregon Sentinel

Lines in Pleasant Places

Science Fiction and Fantasy

by Michael J. Findley

The Empire Saga (all six of the following books in one volume)

City on a Hill and Sojourner (Combined Novella and Short Story)

Nehemiah LLC (Full-length novel available as a standalone ebook, paperback, and hardcover versions)

Empire One: Humiliation

Empire Two: Repentance

Empire Three: Sanctification

Steampunk

by Sophronia Belle Lyon (pen name for Mary C. Findley)

The Alexander Legacy Steampunk Literary Tribute Series

Book One: A Dodge, a Twist, and a Tobacconist (including illustrated version)

Book Two: The Pinocchio Factor

Book Three: The Most Dangerous Game

Book Four: Beware the Bustle

Fantasy/Allegory

by Mary C. Findley

Allegorical clockwork novella inspired by Little Red Riding Hood

The Acolyte's Education

A Paranormal Urban Fantasy serial

His Sign: The Wait Is Over

His Sign 2: The Ezra Solution

Contemporary Fiction

by Mary C. Findley

Romantic Suspense Novella

Fall On Your Knees

Relationships Short Stories

Fifty Shades of Faithful

Fifty Shades of Faithful 2: In Living Color

The Great Thirst Serial Archaeological Mystery (including boxed set of all titles)

Part One: Prepared

Part Two: Purified

Part Three: Pursued

Part Four: Persecuted

Part Five: Persevering

Part Six: Protected

Part Seven: Prevailing

Murder Mystery

Mapped Out Murders

Nonfiction

by Mary C. Findley

Write for the King of Glory, 2nd Edition (updated, with tips on indie writing and publishing)

by Michael J. and Mary C. Findley

The Good, the Bad, and the Ugly: A Readers' and Writers' Guide for Believers

Biblical Studies (Teacher and student editions plus excerpts in OT and NT Manuscript History)

Antidisestablishmentarianism (illustrated and plain versions)

Serial versions, illustrated and plain

What Is an Establishment of Religion?

What Is Secular Humanism?

What Is Science?

What Are the Results of the Establishment of Secular Humanism?

The Conflict of the Ages series (All have teacher and student editions)

I. The Scientific History of Origins

II. The Origin of Evil in the World that Was

III. They Deliberately Forgot: The Flood and the Ice Age

IV. Ice Age Civilizations

V. The Ancient World

by Michael J. Findley

Short Recaps of longer nonfiction works (*Antidisestablishmentarianism* and *Conflict of the Ages*)

Disestablish: An Overview from Creation to the Ice Age

Under the Sun: The Truth about History from the Beginning

*****

Christian Books in Multiple Genres. Join Christian Indie Author ~ Readers Group on Facebook. https://www.facebook.com/groups/291215317668431/

www.ingramcontent.com/pod-product-compliance
Lightning Source LLC
LaVergne TN
LVHW050535160826
845677LV00011B/2045